What Others are Saying about Beautiful Ambition

Tara is an amazing example that no matter how difficult your childhood is… you can still have a warm loving heart, a love of life, and a spiritual light that will guide you into becoming a wonderful person… the kind that Tara has become today!

—*Michael King,* CEO, *King World Productions*

King World is the leading worldwide distributor of first-run programming, including the two highest-rated, first-run strips in syndication, Wheel of Fortune and Jeopardy, OPRAH *(The Oprah Winfrey Show), television's highest-rated syndicated newsmagazine,* Inside Edition, *Dr. Phil, Everybody Loves Raymond, Hollywood Squares The Little Rascals, etc.*

Tara Brooke Boreyko promises that following a precise plan, one she lays out in great detail with all of the dos and don'ts, will bring you "a happy,

i

resilient, and optimistic life." After studying her book, *Beautiful Ambition,* I'm convinced she is right! When you want a guidebook that is spot on with the what's, when's, whys and how's all incorporated in one easy to follow reference, you can't go wrong with *Beautiful Ambition.* Tara shares herself with an innocent vulnerability that is refreshing and encourages trust. If success has a blueprint, Tara is an excellent architect!

—Eldon Taylor, Ph.D. FAPA, Talk Show Host and New York Times
Best Selling Author of Choices and Illusions and Mind Programming

Respected and respectful story-telling, unlocking potential for more, future and success, for EVERYONE! It brings smiles and heart-warming honesty to a willing audience, wanting to make a difference, change and impact.

—Terri Levine Ph.D., Bestselling Author & The Business Mentoring Expert

Every woman can be an extra-ordinary woman, living a LIFE worthy of influence and impact. Unlock YOUR own "Beautiful Ambition" and potential through the stories and down-to-earth advice that Tara weaves together so creatively; she will move and inspire YOU, TOO, with unprecedented humor, candor and insight, as well as providing an action-plan blueprint to follow!

—Debra L. Morrison, International motivational speaker.
MsMorrisonSpeaks.com

Tara masterfully takes readers on an adventure, literally from cover-to-cover, through all meanderings, paths, challenges and opportunities called life! An inspirational, useful book for one-and-all and a definite must-have for your reading, gift and wish list!

—Michael Tasner, Bestselling Author, Marketing In The Moment

I highly recommend Beautiful Ambition for every woman who wants an extraordinary life. No matter what your background may be, Tara's key message is clear—Success is not reserved only for a small, select group of people—it is for every individual who has a dream.

—*Jeanie Buss,* *Executive Vice President, Business Operations of Five Time World Champion Los Angeles Lakers and Author of* Laker Girl

Beautiful Ambition

MY SECRETS TO LOVE, HAPPINESS & SUCCESS

TARA BROOKE

MORGAN JAMES PUBLISHING • NEW YORK

Beautiful Ambition

ISBN: 978-1-60037-978-9 (Paperback)
      978-1-60037-979-6 (eBook)
Library of Congress Control Number: 2011924628

Published by:
MORGAN JAMES PUBLISHING
1225 Franklin Ave Ste 32
Garden City, NY 11530-1693
Toll Free 800-485-4943
www.MorganJamesPublishing.com

Cover/Interior Design by:
Rachel Lopez
rachel@r2cdesign.com

In an effort to support local communities, raise awareness and funds, Morgan James Publishing donates one percent of all book sales for the life of each book to Habitat for Humanity. Get involved today, visit **www.HelpHabitatForHumanity.org.**

I would like to dedicate this book to my wonderful family.

To my mother Linda and my father Timothy… you both mean the world to me!

Thank you for the unconditional love you give to me. You always told me that I could do anything with hard work and dedication and I love you so much. Thank you for believing in me.

To my husband and soul-mate Jason… you really are the true love of my life. I am thankful for every day we get to share together. You are such an inspiration to me. The love and support you have given me, is a true gift! I love this magical adventure we are on! Thank you for our amazing little family.

Finally, to my beautiful children… my son Jaden and my daughter Skye, you are my heart and soul, my greatest blessings and the joy of my life. I am so inspired and motivated by you. Always know that you are loved and adored, that no matter what life throws your way, you can achieve your dreams.

I love you all so much, thank you. Tara

Contents

Foreword

remember meeting Tara in 1997 because she was a beautiful and striking model, motivated and ambitious and truly unforgettable. In 1998 I was surprised to learn she was stepping away from a blossoming career after meeting her future husband Jason. Now, after more than 13 years of marriage and two gorgeous children later, it is no surprise to me that Tara is back in the forefront with a new dream and passion: her mission is to help all women achieve their personal dreams. In her book Beautiful Ambition: My Secrets to Love, Happiness & Success, Tara openly and honestly shares the struggles she dealt with from an early age. Her story is written with great enthusiasm and confidence and it becomes evident that her early years not only served as a training ground on how to survive, but it also helped shape the person she would become.

In Beautiful Ambition Tara provides earnest women, either young or mature, with a step-by-step approach to setting clear goals, ultimately empowering them to obtain their dreams. Her frankness is energizing and her ability to focus on the positive and find gratitude in even the most difficult and challenging situations is truly encouraging. As you are guided along, Tara will inspire and motivate you and from her own *personal* experiences, she will give you key inside tips that can save you time and frustration.

This book is more than just another manual on how to fulfill your desires. It's a real life action plan for self-empowerment and tools for persistence that will bring results. I highly recommend Beautiful Ambition for every woman who wants an extraordinary life. No matter what your background may be, Tara's key message is clear: Success is not reserved only for a small, select group of people—it is for every individual who has a dream. If your vision is not yet clear and you are unsure of the direction you want to take or where to start, this book is bound to push you forward and assist in illuminating your unique path to achieving your goals. Success is out there for anyone willing to work for it!

—Jeanie Buss, Executive Vice President, Business Operations of Five Time World Champion Los Angeles Lakers and Author of Laker Girl

My Life: The Early Years

"Life is the only real counselor; wisdom unfiltered through personal experience does not become a part of the moral tissue."

—*Edith Wharton*

When I decided to write this book, I did it for many reasons. The first reason being that that I felt I had much life-experience and knowledge on these topics to share and a willingness and passion to impart it to others.

I am excited to be sharing my life experiences with you, knowing that YOU may be going through a difficult time now, or you are just starting out and wanting to make excellent choices right from the beginning. It is always easier when you can learn from the mistakes of others, as well as from their triumphs.

Furthermore, I am also drawing from my personal history, life-realities and circumstances, even from an early age onward, which also form part of my journey and life-story.

Throughout my life, I have also always embraced and loved the idea, that I could offer great advice to other people—*even if making a difference, just for one person!*—Which could help them, in turn, then realize their dreams.

Encouragement comes naturally to me and I know that I am at my best when I am living my purpose. I do that by imparting my thoughts and life lessons onto those that have an interest in hearing it. Being able to help others has been and is (for me at least), the real "juice", reward and satisfaction, which for which I live!

This is uniquely consistent with the very person I was while growing up and continue to choose to be today. I was always there to help and at the time, even rescuing others from dangers, harm and risks, giving advice, sound-boarding, guiding, listening*... **I always knew that in some sense, I was an "old soul" and I found comfort in helping out other fellow-travelers!***

Not unlike many of you reading this book, in my childhood, there were challenges. I came from a family that went through a time of trauma during my parents' divorce the years proved to be extremely hard on all of us. I know for myself, there was a lot of sadness, loneliness, as well as extreme financial hardships that placed us in situations where my faith as a very young girl would be put to the test. My mother and I found ourselves moving month to month from one new location and school to the next. For many years there was absolutely no sense of security.

Living that type of lifestyle, I had to grow up and mature quickly, in order to address these and other significant life-challenges, which came my way. Through it all however—*throughout even these very difficult years and troubling times*—I learned so much! **It helped me become who and what I am today.**

For many, the one thing that might be lacking in their lives may very well be LOVE. It's the one true ingredient that can really make or break your life. *Many know its many faces, its relentless sting or its cruel absence…* In my case; LOVE in many ways did in fact turn my life around.

My family was not perfect. There were lots of mistakes along the way, but everyone has things to overcome and challenges to face. However, this is something of key importance—my parents always made sure that I knew that I was loved and they always told me that I could grow up to be anything I wanted to be. They always made me feel special and gave me the confidence that I would need to go after my dreams. I also had a fantastic relationship with both my parents. I just understood them and what we were all going through. Believe me, I *got* it! In fact, today they both play an extremely significant role in my life. My dad is amazing! He is uniquely blessed with an incredible sense of humor. *(No kidding! I like to think I got that from him… ha-ha!).*

On the other hand, my mother is beautiful, tender and loving. We are very close and share a special relationship.

I knew as a young girl that I wanted to have an amazing life. I wanted to travel the world, become a model, marry the handsome prince and live happily ever after. I wanted to live the dream, the fairly-tale life—I wanted it all (and then some!). It was a tall order, I knew even back then, with the odds pretty much stacked against me. However, I always knew and continued to believe that I could do it, reach for and realize it all. This was MY dream, MY life, MY future, MY *reality-to-be*. I would *will* it into being if I had to. I was determined!

Throughout the life-journey in this book, I am going to show you how you, too, can reach for the stars—*how you can become anything you dream of.*

The most important ingredient in all of this is to BELIEVE! It's the ONE difference-maker, to making it all come to pass! *(So stay tuned!)*

Once I entered high school, it was becoming increasingly clear to me that the responsibility for my life-success rested on none other than my own two shoulders. I wasn't going to have anyone get there for me or pave the road on my behalf… and for ME, that road was long and uphill! This journey that lay ahead, this time, was up to me and I knew it. I would have to make it happen, no ifs or buts about it—no-one was going to do it for me.

Looking back on it all, I now know that this was the best thing ever for me. We live in and with a culture of co-dependency and 'entitlement'. So many kids today grow up expecting their parents to do everything for them and they become so dependent on their parents that they can't imagine ever doing 'it' (anything), for and by themselves. Our parents are there to take care of us, love us, feed us and provide a safe place for us. HOWEVER, when it comes to our ideals, our hopes and dreams, we have to reach for them ourselves. That is the long and short of it.

Now, if you are reading this and your family has provided you with a really great launching pad towards realizing your dreams and helps you financially, that is great! Count your blessings and be thankful.

But for those of you that might be able to relate to how it was when I was growing up and my life-story, OR perhaps you might very well be faced with no-one alongside you, nobody looking out for you, or championing and enabling you (like many others—you are NOT alone!), there is hope, I assure you. Take heart! Know that hard work and dedication WILL get you there.

YOU CAN DO IT!
YOU HAVE TO BELIEVE IN YOURSELF!

You need that vision and reminder in your mind every day of your life. Focus on wanting and starting to plan out how you are going to achieve it.

I know that when I turned sixteen, I bought my first car! I worked forty hours a week at Long's drug store, went to high school riding the bus until I had enough money for my car. Later, I then also held down a second job at night and on weekends, waiting tables, to get ahead and make ends meet, while working to reach for my dream. I did whatever it took and made it work.

I went to a performing arts high school to learn about all the things I loved deeply and dearly. This included dance, drama and music. I was an average, to 'okay' student. I was always daydreaming about my future, my tomorrows, and my life after school, so I did have a hard time staying focused.

I did not want to go to college. I wanted to graduate and move to Los Angeles and hit the ground running. I stayed out of trouble in high school, mostly because I worked all the time and that kept me away from the parties. Also, I was not really interested in being the social butterfly in school.

Having lived through the taunts of kids growing up, various forms of bullying and ridicule, when things were really difficult, these events actually opened my eyes to the realities and challenges in school, so for me it was all about getting out and moving on with my life.

I really only had one boyfriend in eleventh grade and we dated for a while. I lived with my dad and he was so adamant about me NOT dating, it was as if he felt like getting a boyfriend would keep me from reaching my goals. The one thing that was always important to me was showing my parents that I could make it. I wanted to make them proud.

Life was not easy for them and I wanted to show them that I could do anything I set my mind to. Believe me, I was not a perfect angel, but for the most part I did stay out of trouble and I really never "rebelled". I had a clearly defined goal… to ensure that I would graduate and move to Los Angeles and that's EXACTLY what I did! After years of waiting, I was finally ready to make it happen!

I moved to Los Angeles and got an apartment. I had just enough money saved up to last me about 12 months if I was careful. This would give me the time I needed to get out there and get settled, find work and be well on my way to living my dream.

My first order of business was securing an agency and getting my portfolio together. I found a reasonable photographer that had worked with tons of models. He shot most of my first book I created. I had my ticket and now I was off to the races!

I started going out on auditions right away. This industry is not for the faint of heart. You cannot decide that you want to be a model and not get rejected. Rejection is the main ingredient in the modeling recipe and process. You simply have to be able to understand and look at it realistically from that perspective. The bottom line is that IF you are *just not "the look" they are going for*, maybe your look will be the right-fit for the next one. ***You keep going...***

Los Angeles is full of pit-falls and traps. If you are a beautiful young woman the world is yours, but it also comes with a heavy price to pay if you are not careful.

When living and working in fast-paced Los Angeles, the same rules apply.

You simply cannot allow yourself to get distracted with the night life and the men, because that element is all around you. It is pervasively everywhere you turn or go. Do not get me wrong! I had my share of fun! I loved going to parties.

I had my foot in the door at all the right spots and I loved every minute of it. But I also had to take care of myself FIRST, so it was important that I was up early, working out, looking good and ready to go at the drop of a hat. At these types of auditions you cannot and will not get hired if/when you are hung over.

Staying focused on why you are there is of the utmost importance. I landed my first magazine cover in the first sixty days. I felt so happy and I had a real sense of accomplishment and purpose. It made it real to me and I felt like I could do anything! My modeling career seemed to be taking off and it was turning a corner into the fitness and swimsuit arena (which I loved).

Having to stay in bikini-shape year-round helped me stay committed to working out and eating right. I met some amazing people along the way. Soon I started to make a lot of money and good money at that! I had really changed my life for the better and I was beginning to achieve my dreams.

As time passed and things progressed for me, I had steady covers and layouts and I started to work in front of the camera as a spokesperson, which I really loved. Others were throwing words like 'icon', role model and such around. It was so much fun too.

I was able to travel, meet great people and have a new set of opportunities and challenges to take full advantage of, embracing being a significant part of it all. It was right around the time that I was starring in three of my own workout tapes, that I would meet my Prince Charming.

Let me tell you ladies; do NOT listen to the women that say they don't exist, because they do!

I had just turned twenty-three years old. I was independent and taking care of myself. To top it off, I had reached my goal to be a working model and now a spokeswoman that others could look up to—others to whom I could now lend a voice, where they have had none before.

In fact, I was working as a spokes-model for a business that had created a diet product for another organization. *(The latter owned by my very-soon-to-be husband!)*.

My boss had asked me to fly into Las Vegas for a meeting with some-or-other nutrition company. He said that they wanted to meet me. Well, when I walked into the Bally's hotel for the meeting, a very tall and extremely handsome guy came up to me and said: "Are you in our group?"

I affirmed and said yes. He then escorted me to the table at the restaurant where we would all be meeting. He seated me right across from him and throughout the course of the meeting, he kept kicking my foot. Of course every time he did this, I would look up and smile, so he was clearly getting the response he wanted. *(Long after I found out that my boss was trying to play match maker between the two of us. Of course I had no inkling or idea of any of this, until much later!)*.

Jason asked for my number and then several weeks later we set up our first date. There were a few things that gave me enough reason to pause and look before I leapt! The reality is, I really liked him, but was I ready for a committed relationship? Perhaps I was just a little afraid to commit so soon after just starting on my success-path in life, realizing my dream, pursuing my professional career-goals? Challenges sure! All relationships have them, but for me, there were many positives! Some initial concerns and hurdles kept harping and nagging at us (probably mostly me!), like:

What stage of life was I in? What were my needs? What about Jason and his needs, wants and desires? Is this what I needed at this point in my life (or not?)

There was also the fact that I was not really looking to be in a serious relationship at all, let alone a long-distance connection. Personally and professionally, I had just started on this road to success, inching ahead and my blossoming dream-career was beginning to really take off. For all intents and purposes, I did not want the distraction.

Another complicating factor (for me) was that Jason lived in Arizona and I lived in Los Angeles. How was that going to work when we both had really busy lives? But, today I can tell you this… Jason pursued me with great determination and there were times that I did not make it easy on him.

I basically had the man of my dreams right before my eyes and I almost let him get away or fall through my fingers.

The good news is that it all turned out incredibly well in the end. We started dating exclusively soon after. He would come out on weekends, or I would fly there. It worked well for the two of us, this long-distance relationship-thing.

We were dating only thirty days, when on the evening of February 13th Jason had invited me down to his company's event. (I suspected NOTHING!). When I came into the room, he had rented the Presidential Suite.

The room was stocked with beautiful bouquets of flowers—purple roses and white Casablanca's (my favorite). They were all over—myriads of them! The fire was on, with the room romantically lit by candles. There were butlers in tuxedos waiting for me with champagne. I walked in innocently thinking: *"Oh my gosh! This guy is the most romantic guy I have ever met! I can not believe he is going all out like this for Valentine's Day,* "(which incidentally was the next day!).

I had no idea that it would be the night that he would propose to me. We went out on the balcony lit with long white candles and flowers, when he told me something along the lines of: *"I was the girl of his dreams and that he loved me and wanted to spend the rest of his life with me and would I marry him."*

My head was spinning. It took me what must have felt like an eternity to him, to answer his question, BUT finally I did reply and said, "Yes, I will marry you!" So, there it was. That was it! Everything from that moment on seemed like a dream—the perfect dream! My dream! We were married on March 1st, just two weeks later, in front of our family and friends, at a black-tie wedding at the Ritz Carlton in Pasadena, CA, USA. It was incredible. It was a fairy tale come true!

Jason had an amazing team (mostly his incredible assistant at the time who is now like family to me) that helped us plan the most incredible wedding. We pulled it off and it was perfect. I wore a Vera Wang gown and I truly felt like Cinderella. After our honeymoon in Hawaii, we found our home in Newport Beach, CA, USA, where we still live today.

Now fast forward a bit… we are close to celebrating our 13th year anniversary as husband and wife and we have two amazing twins, our son Jaden Brooks and our darling angel daughter Skye Isabela. They bring us so much joy our family is complete and I can tell you that dreams do come true. Your past does not matter!

What matters is what you decide to change, how you push forward, ever-moving ahead, you are the only one that can truly define your life and how happy you will be.

In this book, I will show you the very best ways to utilize what gifts you do have and help you lay out a plan for success. I want you to take courage, be motivated, and inspire you along the way as we journey together. It is my deepest wish that everyone reading this book will be blessed and has all of the desires of their own heart.

Remember, we are all here with our own goals. They are all as different as the roads that we take and the decisions we make. All of these have their impact, costs and consequences—*some working for the better and some towards the not so great*. What makes life so enriched with possibilities and opportunities are considering both paths while navigating your way through life.

Both of these life-paths—while learning along the way—keeping your faith and loving the people in your life, will keep catapulting you forward. The journey itself matters just as much, if not more, than only the destination!

Although at times while on the path of life, the going can seem difficult, this is what reaps the most rewards. You can never stop learning, and if you commit to the challenges and principles I have laid out for you in the book you will be in the position to harvest great success in your lifetime.

So, now that you know a little more about me, let us continue this journey together and get to the real reason you are reading this book and that is… it is all about you! So, let us have some fun, discover what that means and where it will take you!

Chapter 2

I Want it All and I Want it All Now

"Life takes on meaning when you become motivated, set goals and charge after them in an unstoppable manner."

—Les Brown

E xperts and women like you share simple tips for landing whatever your heart desires, whether it's comfy shoes or your share of the American pie. But sometimes knowing—really knowing—what YOU want, is the hardest part of all!

What further complicates this process for all women, I think, is our capacity for empathy... our penchant for caretaking. Yes, the way we can't seem to be truly satisfied unless we are doing something for someone else, someone other than ourselves.

I find myself wanting to save and rescue those around me and I always have to remind myself that I can only do so much and that the people I love are themselves responsible for their lives and their actions.

This doesn't, however, mean that you become unwilling to help when you can. Nevertheless, there is a big difference between helping a loved one out and trying to save or rescue them from their choices.

Our generous nature is oftentimes the very best thing about us, but we run into trouble if this very generosity turns into martyrdom and resentment. This is exactly when our good intentions toward those we love, deafen us to that quieter call of our own desires. We all have to stay focused on our own dream(s) and understand that we count, and our own life matters also and very much so!

Following a heart's desire involves risks. Whether starting your own business, falling in love, writing fiction, running a marathon for the first time… You have to try your hand at it, and you have to be willing to fail.

In my life I have had many "failed or less successful attempts", and to be really brutally honest, it truly makes the times that much sweeter when I win or hit the mark, goal or target that I've set out for myself to achieve or out-perform.

After all, how can I possibly write a book on reaching your own dreams, if I do not understand the pain and disappointment that comes with failing or falling short of that very dream? Yes, it is that acknowledgement that empowers and engages others! Yes, it can and does happen to us all! However, they say, *"It's not how hard you fall it's how high you bounce back"*. **(I have become the master of bouncing back and so will you!).**

Understand that life is about pressing on and finding the joy in the journey even though the journey is challenging, or the going gets tough. You can always find and see the positive in every situation. Believe me, by having this kind of attitude, you will become more inspired and motivated to work harder, despite any setbacks you may or may not experience.

After all the soul-searching, second-guessing and the final banishment of lingering doubt, the execution of these plans can seem like the easy part.

Once you let yourself know that what you really want is to start a catering business, you head to Kinko's for business cards and flyers, check the want ads for kitchen space, and call up those rich friends who always rave about your cooking and see how much they would like to invest. If you've always wanted to write a novel but have three kids under 6, look into day care, call in a favor from your sister, and set the alarm for 3 a.m.

Here is the crux of the matter: Don't let hard work or a tough schedule keep you from going after your dreams.

It does get easier and you will be come "luckier" as you start hitting your marks because you will begin working in a positive flow with a plan of action. When this happens, things start falling into place. You will start attracting the very things into your life, with enabled positive thinking, affirming type speech, and by deliberate action!

We have the right, the tools, and the capacity, to live precisely the lives we want to. We are the generation of doers, the gender that lifts cars off of babies, wins the Iditarod, and swims the English Channel, after all! Anyone who gets in the way of our heart's desire once we have really made up our minds, better watch out!

A GREAT EXAMPLE: ANGELINA JOLIE

One person who knew what she wanted, set goals for herself, and most certainly attained and exceeded them, is Angelina Jolie.

One great example of a woman learning who she is and following her dreams and values along the path she feels is right for her, is Jolie. Though she is the daughter of famous actor Jon Voight, her parents divorced when she was only a year old, and she was raised exclusively by her mother in Palisades, New York, while her father remained on the opposite side of the country. She went to the movies regularly with her mother and older brother, and states that this was what interested her in acting (not her father and/or his legacy, influence or profession of choice).

With this decision made, and a convenient move by her family to Los Angeles, Angelina enrolled at *The Lee Strasberg Theatre Institute* where she trained for two years and appeared in several stage productions. Even though she felt like an outsider throughout her school years (especially at Beverly Hills High School), being teased for her different looks, skinniness, braces, and second-hand clothing, her cinematic ambitions continued to grow and blossom.

She took a stab at modeling, but was wholly unsuccessful, decreasing her self-confidence quite dramatically. This caused her to become unhappy, feeling worthless, and beginning a dangerous self-mutilation habit of cutting herself.

She dropped out of acting classes at the age of fourteen and instead, dreamed of becoming a funeral director—a darker pursuit that matched her self-loathing and black clothing. She moved in with her boyfriend, but seemed to know deep in her heart that acting was something she needed. She returned to theatre after graduating from high school. From that time onward, her acting career grew gradually, and reached blockbuster-hit status.

However, Angelina was never one to let life pass on blindly around her. While filming the first *Lara Croft* movie in Cambodia, Angelina was struck by the poverty-stricken and widely-minded nation. This opened her eyes to an entirely different side of the world, and a new cause was added to Angelina's priorities.

Since 2001, Angelina has worked hard both in promoting humanitarian causes and her work with refugees, through the UNHCR.

She has been a UNHCR Goodwill Ambassador since that time, and earned recognition for her work with the first *Citizen of the World Award* by the United Nations Correspondents Association. Jolie has also been awarded Cambodian citizenship by its King Norodom Sihamoni for the conservation work she did in August of 2005. In October of that year, she was awarded the UNA-USA Global Humanitarian Award. Today, we all know her as a super-star American personality and celebrity-royalty. But, what about before all this fairy-tale living on top of the world? What is her real story? *Note: (For more on Angelina Jolie's life-story, read: "Angelina: An Unauthorized Biography" by Andrew Morton, (released August, 2010), amidst all the other things she does, make movies, do charity work, being a mother and parent full-time, and so much more!)*

From playing roles like the blockbuster "Lara Croft" series, to off-camera international charity projects, (refugee-work with UN), she often tops lists of most accomplished, trend-setting, philanthropic, or "most beautiful women" type characterizations. The lists are literally endless and growing as we speak, too numerous to list even try to list here! *(she will be present, if not at the top, close to, or under the first lot, to be sure!)*

As mentioned earlier, she was very young when exposed to a professional career in modeling. Her exotic beauty is an asset that still carries her career today. Films and critical acclaim followed (still does), with Golden Globes, Emmys, SAG and Academy Awards, for best leading actress in a supporting role to her name, to name but a few.

Headlining with the best, like Denzel Washington and Winona Ryder, her personal life, relationships and marriages sent her life on a rollercoaster. This included failed marriages to co-stars Jonny Lee Miller and Billy Bob Thornton both of which ended in divorce, as well as the well-published speculated affair between her and Brad Pitt, that led to the break-up of Jennifer Aniston and Pitt. Estrangements and brief rapprochements between father and daughter formed part of her life, history and being, all part of the more private side of Jolie's life.

There is, however, this undeniably large humanitarian contribution and portion to Jolie's private and public life that needs special mention here. From visiting refugee camps, stints as the Goodwill Ambassador for the United Nations High Commissioner for Refugees (UNHCR) are captured in her book entitled" Notes from My Travels" (all profits of which go to UNHCR) and philanthropic undertakings globally, she is an advocate for humanity, charity and reaching out to others.

She wants to be a full-time mom and is often still called the sexiest woman alive and continues to do amazing work with and for those children orphaned by AIDS. She insists on performing her own stunts with a real bleeding and philanthropic heart for others, (for example giving her Oscar Statuette, Golden Globes, SAG Awards, and Critic Choice Award to her mother, not really seeing value in holding onto them!).

Her work-ethic and personal commitment is impeccable. She is driven, and gets results. She is also one of the first actresses to win three consecutive Golden Globes in three different categories: *"Best Supporting Actress in a Mini Series": George Wallace (1997) (TV), "Best Actress in a TV Movie or Mini Series": Gia (1998) (TV), "Best Supporting Actress in a Motion Picture": Girl, Interrupted (1999).*

From sex-symbol to top-celebrity, smart, accomplished and beautiful, her name is always on the top of some ratings-list or person/people's lists and favorites. Forbes Magazine estimated her earnings for the year at $20 million, in 2007.

She is left-handed, pilot's small airplanes and loves soccer, donating many items to charity for fundraising. She suffered immense grief and loss when her mother Marcheline Bertrand died, (battling ovarian cancer for over seven and a half years, in 2007). Yes, nothing much stops or deters Jolie. When the rules said she could not adopt a little boy because she and Pitt were not a married couple, she adopted Pax as a single parent (with Brad Pitt then later domestically adopting his son, when back on US soil)!

Angelina came to know the joys of motherhood again when she herself gave birth to twins, a boy and a girl on July 12, 2008 in Nice, France: Knox Léon, and Vivienne Marcheline Jolie-Pitt. Again her tenacity and personal commitment showed (only eight months after giving birth to her twins) when she returned to work full-time to film Salt, just released in the summer of 2010. (This was no different than when she insisted on returning to work with that strong work ethic and dedication, only four months after giving birth to her daughter Shiloh back in 2007!). She was two months pregnant with twins Knox and Vivienne when she completed filming on Changeling (2008) and six months pregnant with her daughter Shiloh while completing filming on The Good Shepherd (2006).

In Angelina's own words…

"Because I am a bad girl, people always automatically think that I am a bad girl. Or that I carry a dark secret with me or that I'm obsessed with death. The truth is that I am probably the least morbid person one can meet. If I think more about death than some other people, it is probably because I love life more than they do."

If you don't get out of the box you've been raised in, you won't understand how much bigger the world is.

I was actually quite a cool kid. I was not tough. I was certainly independent and bold. I was never teased. I never had any trouble from anybody. … I was never satisfied. I had trouble sleeping. I didn't really fit. I always feel that I'm searching for something deeper, something more… You want to meet other people that challenge you with ideas or with power or with passion. I wanted to live very fully. I wanted to live many lives and explore many things."

Angelina Jolie is a true role-model for people looking to discover how important it is to know themselves. For me personally, I am inspired by her ability to take a leap of faith and get involved with the UN, knowing that she would have to learn a lot quickly and hands-on! She is not deferred or deterred easily—she just rocks on, moving forward! I like that…

She decided to study everything she could about the issues she would be facing. She has flown all around the world in an effort to be there to see it first hand and then go back to Washington and fight for other peoples' needs. She has reminded me that there are people all around the world that you can touch, IF you take the time to learn about it and find something that you are passionate about, wanting to make a difference and impact. I think that the steps she has taken, have redirected her life in a positive way <u>and</u> have given her BOTH purpose and self-confidence.

WHAT DO YOU WANT?

"Make your life a mission-not an intermission."

—*Arnold H. Glasgow*

Choice. It's all about freedom—the freedom to choose and make better decisions, prioritizing and picking one thing over another. Stop to consider this key question: "Are you choosing what you want from life?"

"Oh no," comes the reply. "I can't because… I haven't got enough education… I need to look after my family… I don't have enough money… I don't have the time."

So, let me not mince words and ask you point-blank: What's YOUR excuse?

All of the things listed above were also issues that I have had to deal with and address myself to. Hard to believe? Yes, but it is true! After all, I have only a high school degree, I came from a family that had financial challenges while I was growing up (that is, we were downright poor!), and if I would have listened to negative people around me or even my own fear, I could NEVER have gotten this far, or even brought myself to anywhere near were I am at today. The reality: excuses, just like debilitating fear, will grind you to a halt robbing you of your very hopes and dreams.

The truth is that we have choices every single moment of our lives. For those who are destitute however, the choices in life are less, fewer and far between (if at all!). But, as for the rest of us… let us set the record straight for once! **WE often think we don't have freedom when we simply haven't claimed our power to choose differently!**

How do you typically make decisions? *Do you do so, based on…*

- **"shoulds"**—doing what you believe you should do.

- **pleasing others**—doing what others want or expect you to do.

- **fear**—choosing the safe route for fear of doing something different.

- **habit and reaction**—you don't even think about what you're doing—you've always done it this way?

On the other hand, you own your power to choose... *When you decide on the basis of...*

- **desire**—choosing something you want

- **need**—responding to deeper desires

- **authenticity**—you know who you are and what you stand for

- **creative expression**—you strive to be more.

So how can you be open to choosing 'differently' and BETTER? For once, be clear about what it is that you DO want. Have a sense of purpose. **With a target to aim for, you'll know what will serve you best.**

Here is something you will find very interesting! It should forever drive this point home. Thousands of Harvard Graduates get this wrong every year ... and pay the price! (See if you know the answer!)...

What's the ONE step you must take in order to ensure that you will get what you really want from your life? Not just financial wealth, but great relationships, lifestyle, spiritual wealth, and happiness? If you know, write it down! (*97% of Harvard Graduates blow this question every year!*)

Here's Why!! Harvard doesn't teach it! LIFE DOES! In fact, you will NOT find this in the course catalog for any college and it would be very unusual to find this in the course work at the high school level, yet it is glaringly and obviously 'ABSENT'. Your parents or friends probably don't know the answer either. Maybe it is just too simple: One amazingly simple little step!!!

3% of Harvard Graduates took one simple step, did ONE thing a little... DIFFERENTLY! The ONE thing that the other 97% didn't do or think about... This resulted in a BIG difference and will continue to differentiate success and exceed expectations. Because of this, they not only made more money than the 97% combined, but they lived happier, healthier, more successful lives, both personally and professionally.

> **NOTE:** *These numbers are from a study tens of thousands of Harvard graduates back in the 60's. (It's been repeated a couple of times with similar results).*

This **_One Amazingly Simple Step_** that really successful people take, is to plan their lives in detail on paper (to start)... AND THEN, they actually work their plan. And when I say detail—I mean **EVERY** detail. They wrote down a plan for every aspect of their lives and then they went after it. ***Step, by step, by step***!!

Now let us get down to business! Here is a tough question for you. *Are you working someone else's plan for your life?* If you are **NOT** getting what you want from life, it is probably because you have allowed someone else to design your life plan. This could be your parents, your spouse, your boss, the government, even your friends that might oblige and be happy to plan and map your life FOR you. BUT, this is not the fast track to success—if anything, it is the slow boat to mediocrity. Success is a *do-it-to-yourself* proposition that comes from designing the life you want and deserve and then taking significant action to achieve it.

Can You Learn The Life Planning Skills Of The Top 3%—You Bet!!!

Stop and ask yourself in-depth get-real type questions, like: *"Why am I doing this? What do I want to achieve?"*

Write down your answers. Use your journal. *Get in the habit of carrying and using your journal as a success tool. Be more conscious of how you are spending your precious time, because this is your life passing by. This will help you start to recognize where you're doing well, and when you are headed down the wrong path altogether. I spend a good amount of my time writing out what I wanted, because it helps me stay focused on the goal* *every day. I look at it and I know how I am going to spend my time that day.*

I also like to add pictures to my journal of things that I want or would love to accomplish. That way I can see them when I open it up. So next time you see something that catches your eye, tear it out and paste in your journal. The more you think about it by visualizing and putting the right action-steps to work, the faster you will have whatever you are reaching for. It really is that simple!

Never allow yourself to play the 'victim' or be victimized. Victims have given away all of their power. Remember: YOU alone are responsible for your life! When you fully accept this, you will claim your enabling inner-power to make BETTER choices. Change often comes from nothing more than a shift in perspective.

When I look back at the many different challenges I had while growing up, I am thankful that these things came across my path on my life-journey. I am such a stronger person now. I have confidence in my ability to persevere. I know that whatever life throws my way, I can move mountains! That knowledge comes from looking at your past experiences and realizing that you are now in control and no matter what happens, YOU alone can create your future.

I want to encourage you to **step out with confidence and really give it your all.** DO NOT let ANYBODY stand in your way! A *'victim'* mentality will typically keep great people from coming into your life. Only YOU can decide to stop being a victim and **start living today**!

Be open to possibilities for yourself. *Select one area of your life where you are unsatisfied, and choose something new, something more for yourself. Do different things and do things differently. Risk more.*

SETTING GOALS AND ACHIEVING THEM

The best fundamental psychological tool for achieving the best results from your life, is to set SMART goals (S-specific, M-Measurable, A-Attainable,

R-Realistic, T-Timely) <u>and</u> knowing HOW to follow through on achieving those goals. *(SIDE-BAR: like I mentioned in Chapter 1, I always write out my goals in the morning of every day. Try it with your journal. Put down* **everything** *you want for your life).*

In theory, setting goals is a very easy task. For example, *"I want learn to play the guitar."* However, as great as that goal is, it **DOES NOT** provide you with a way in which to achieve your aim.

The following is a guideline that can help you achieve your goals:

- State your goal as a **positive statement** ("do", instead of "don't") example: *"I will earn $150,000 a year"* instead of *"I won't make less money than I deserve."*

- Be **precise** about your goal (*state dates, and a measurable amount of achievement so that you can know when you have achieved your goal*).

- Set **priorities** (*so that when you have several goals, you won't feel overwhelmed, you'll know which ones are the most important*).

- **Write** your goals down (*this solidifies them and makes them feel more important*).

- Keep your **operational goals small** (*having many smaller goals is better than one large goal, since it's easier to see your progress and stay motivated*).

- Instead of setting an outcome, set a **performance goal** (*this way, there is a control factor to your achievement. Nothing is more dispiriting than failing due to reasons beyond your control, such as bad business environments, or just plain bad luck*).

- Be **realistic** about your goals (*set goals that you can achieve, and don't be influenced by others who try to set goals beyond your abilities. You* *can always set another goal if you discover that your first goal was not reaching high enough).*

- Don't set your **goals too low** *(otherwise, you will slow down your progress, become lazy, and simply won't achieve your maximum potential).*

- When you do achieve one of your goals, make certain that you have taken the time to enjoy the satisfaction of having accomplished your desire, by allowing yourself a **well deserved break or reward.** *(It can be as small as an afternoon off to go see that movie you have wanted to see).*

- It is also important to make certain to absorb the **implications** of the achievement of your goal, and have a look back at the **progress** you have made. You should also look at the progress that you have made towards other goals. If the goal was especially noteworthy, make sure that you reward yourself appropriately.

Through the experience of having achieved your goal, take a look at the rest of your goal plans:

- If your goal was achieved with too much simplicity, and provided you with little profit, **make sure that you aim a little higher next time**, and **take more risks to expand your opportunities.**

- If your goal can't seem to get off the ground, and you find yourself becoming dispirited, this could be because the goal you have set is beyond your reach or doesn't interest you. If this occurs, it's **time for you to pursue a new goal.**

- If you've learned something along the way to achieving your first goal that would lead you to **change your second goal—change it!**

If, while you achieved your goal, you noticed that one (or a few) of your skills are lacking, decide if you should be **setting new goals to remedy this.** Remember, just because you don't meet your goals doesn't mean that you haven't been successful. You can **learn from the experience**, and work these lessons into your future goal-setting program.

- You may also choose to **change your deadline** if you find that you are not able to meet your goal by the time you had originally planned. *(I have done this so many times. If it's something that is important to me, I just stay focused and change the date if I have to. Just remember to maintain that focus, and not get too lax with the date. You may have to change the date, but you still have to get there!).*

Moreover, your goals will change with your experiences and as your skills develop. Therefore, you should adjust your goals regularly so that they reflect the targets that you wish to achieve.

It is important that your goals continue to hold an attraction for you, otherwise, you will not be motivated to continue to seek them out. If your goals do not attract you anymore, let them go, and set a new one. A goal should bring you pleasure and satisfaction, and a sense of achievement when you have attained it.

Another great way to achieve a goal as Steven Covey says *"is to begin with the end in mind"*. A successful ambition needs a focused goal. Therefore, think about what you are aiming to accomplish and go after it.

The fact remains that no matter what your goal, to get there you have to start correctly, by beginning with the end in mind. It is so counter-intuitive. If you are not doing this, then you are only wandering aimlessly. If you do not know where you are going, any road will take you there. As yourself: *"Where am I trying to go with all of my efforts?"*

If you are unable to answer this question, you will not be able to get very far... simply because you will not know the best way to achieve your goal, nor will you recognize it once you have accomplished it.

Therefore, to make sure that you're always making your best progress, ask yourself where you are trying to be and get to, keeping your eye on your goal. If you do not know the answer to the question: *"Where am I trying to go with all of my efforts?"*, then your top priority right now, is to consider it with intent and deliberate engagement, doing so UNTIL you can come up with a reasonable answer—to which you can then set your goals.

This may require a great deal of thought, where you need to ponder it for a length of time, reflecting (lying down with your eyes closed if you have to, to NOT be distracted!), OR you may find that it is an answer that comes naturally to you, but you had just never considered it before.

Take out your journal and just scribble, scratch and 'doodle' in it. Draw freely and express yourself. That tends to open up the right side (more creative side) of your brain. It will stimulate and generate creative ideas that you can ponder and consider, from different perspectives. **Remember, your journal is a powerful tool. Use it to its fullest capacity and possibilities!**

It is NOT vital that your answer to the question be <u>*absolutely perfect.*</u> After all, you can always alter or change your answer as you progress. But if you don't have a goal in the first place, you will not know whether or not it is right or wrong for you.

You WILL NOT be able to answer these critical questions:

- *How are you going to get there?*

- *What is your plan?*

- *Is it a good plan?*

- *How do you know it's a good plan?*

- *Are you sure?*

- *Every day are you doing something to get you closer to the end?*

I know the power of writing goals has proved invaluable for me and this is something that I do now… ***and will continue doing for the rest of my life***. Let this be a new habit that you learn to stick with. I promise that not only will it help you reach your goals, but you will also learn so much about yourself along the way!

Never underestimate the power you have over your own fate. You are in control of your own future. Stay focused, and keep the end in mind as you take action, and **YOU WILL** get there!

> **TIP:** Here is a technique I still use to this day. I take 2 different sets of colored 3x5 cards. On one of the colored set of cards, I write down my short-term goals. I use green colored ones for these (as it represents to me what is happening now). You can use whatever colors you want.

On the other set of colored cards I write down my long-term goals. Then I tape them to my bathroom mirror, where I can see them each and every morning.

Some mornings I stop to read and think about them. Other mornings I just let my subconscious mind absorb them and go about my morning routine. This is a very powerful way to keep you on track. It also allows your sub-conscious mind to work in the background on other, new, more and/or different ways to achieve your goals. This is sometimes known as the "ah-ha" moment. Try it. It will have a tremendous impact on all aspects of your life.

Furthermore, motivation and confidence are two of the most essential *"thinking like a winner"* basics that can also really help your goals and you achieving success. They can easily be enforced through an extremely simple concept known as *positive self-talk.*

Positive self-talk is a tremendously powerful utility you can rely on to help you out. It is used by many people and works no matter what the situation, regardless of how good or bad it seems. All you have to do is talk to and tell yourself why things are not as bad as they appear, and inform yourself how you plan to and will fix things.

I do this all the time when I find myself in any unfamiliar situation. I take a minute to think it through, by talking to myself, giving my *'self'* the emotional support that I need. (*Every day, I tell myself that I am achieving my dreams and that good things happen to me; that people like me, and that I am making a difference*).

So many times, we self-sabotage ourselves. DO NOT be afraid of the power that you have to be great. I know that it can be scary to have success fall into your life this easily because of fear, but self-sabotage does happen a lot, tripping up many along the way. **However, by using positive self-talk, you will recognize whether or not you are sabotaging your own progress.**

Here are a few examples of the things that I say everyday to **affirm** *myself*. These might seem simplistic, yet they are powerfully effective!

Try repeating the following to yourself:

- *I am achieving my dreams and desires every day. I am a success.*

- *I like myself and what I see when I look in the mirror. I am a good person.*

- *I make friends easily and people like me.*

- *I make great financial decisions.*

- *I am in the best shape of my life.*

- *My body is healthy and strong*

- *My mind is alert and sharp.*

- *I can do all things*

DO NOT mock it, until you have tried it! Yes, they are simplistic and if you say the words, and believe them—no matter how bad the situation is, no matter how you got yourself there—YOUR mind will be working to get you out of it! This happens by YOU telling yourself that everything is fine, and it will all be over soon. (This is not denial or wishful thinking—it is affirmation, followed by deliberate, empowered action!).

Naturally, the above-mentioned example is not the only words you can use for self-talking/self-speak or inner-monologue. **You should make up your own words to repeat that work for you, for your personal mantra, for any bad situation that you can think of.**

Be honest with (i) yourself <u>and</u> (ii) about ANY 'issue' that you may face, whether positive or negative. This is where you can be real and truthful. No one will judge you, because this is a completely private matter. Therefore, you can think about the things that you need to hear. Make a list, and repeat it to yourself every day. Love yourself and start building your own self-esteem. This positive *self-talk* is also not limited to bad situations. It can make advantageous positions even better.

When coming up with positive *self-talk* phrases, think of a good situation as well as one of the worst situations that you can come up with. As you think up each situation, **try to create two or three phrases that can encourage you to do much better.** Next, test them out when you take risks and put your goal into action to see if/how they work.

If you find that they are NOT quite doing the trick, just **keep thinking up new phrases and practice them**, until you discover the best one for you.

If you are NOT yet using positive *self-talk*, those people who are using it have a substantial advantage over you. Only YOU can change this fact. These are the people who are taking advantage of a powerful universal reality: *the spoken word.*

Every successful person in the world knows this, and therefore incorporates positive self-speak, enabling inner-monologue, into his or her ambitions in some form or another, ***because they know it works!***

THE POWER OF VISUALIZATION

Use the powerful tool of visualization to help you imagine with your minds-eye what your dreams and goals are… and then think about it all the time. Keep it front of mind.

Take time every day to do this. Find a quiet space were you can be alone to **dream and imagine everything you want for your life**. (Maybe take out your personal journal and do a little doodling—creative self-expression).

Focus on the dream becoming a reality. DARE TO DREAM! Fantasize about it. This is what I did throughout my childhood. I would go into my thought, possibilities and mind-world to then dream about a great life. Use that incredible imagination that you have to create your future! Once you know what you want to do, then you can focus on the details on how to make it happen!

> **SIDE-BAR:** An example where this worked exceptionally well for me would be… when I was out of high school I knew that I wanted to move to L.A. and I had a dream to be a model but I had to really focus on what steps I needed to take to make that happen.

Of course, that meant working, saving money, <u>and</u> staying on my course, so that I could really give myself a chance. It took time and I had to work at jobs that really did not like, (not unlike the rest of the world!). However, when I became frustrated, I would think about my goal and remind myself why I had to stay on track. I had days that I wanted to quit! We all do! It is normal, so do NOT beat yourself up—just remember that you will have good days and bad days.

Life is a game of trade-offs, of give and take. You want one thing, but in order to get it, you have to give up something else. *(You will discover which goals are really important to you when this happens. Just be aware and everything will work out).*

When you have a bad day, allow yourself to have that bad day. Not wallowing in it, but telling yourself, affirming, that in the morning it will be great and you will wake up renewed and excited about your path. Thinking about what you want, combined with the words you use <u>and</u> writing out your goals, will change your life. **It works, trust me on that! Just look at my life!**

As you can see, there are many ways in which you can realize your goals successfully. All of the tools already exist within you. You simply need to discover, uncover, and make the most of them. You need to have the courage to use them POWERFULLY and DIFFERENTLY!

Remember, you're the only one who can make or break your success —begin with the end in mind, trust your instincts and go for it!

WHAT YOU SHOULD LEARN FROM THIS CHAPTER

Key-reminders and insights from Chapter 2, highlight:

- Women often struggle to find the **balance between natural generosity and following their heart's desire** to achieve personal/ professional dreams and goals.

- Following your dream(s) begins with **understanding what you truly want from life.**

- **Goals** are only achieved when you take certain efforts to set them, and then achieve them. *(This includes many important techniques such as defining your goal with specificity and having a clear strategy for attaining the goal).*

- Your odds of achieving your goal greatly increase when you **write them down**. *(This causes you to articulate your goals, and gives you a clear, specific, and real statement of what you want, and how you'll get there).*

- Never underestimate the value of **positive *self-talk***. You'll avoid self-sabotage, while giving yourself the advantage you need to overcome any obstacles that may appear in your way.

- Use **visualization** to create your future. Focus on the things that you want to achieve and spend time thinking about them. Find time each day to be still and think about all the things that you want in life and use this precious time to help guide you through the steps it will take, to get the results you want

Now let's continue…

Chapter 3

Who Am I?

"The final mystery is oneself."

—Oscar Wilde

This is one topic that you do not study in school, even though it is the one subject that is the most important to your happiness <u>and</u> quality of life, as long as you live. *You* are the most exciting study you'll ever take on. The BETTER you get to know yourself and find out what an incredible person you truly are, *(i) the more prepared you will be to understand others, (ii) able to make sound choices for your lifestyle and career, (iii) discovering meaning in your life, and (iv) create your own personal happiness.*

However, finding out <u>who you are</u> and <u>what you want from your life,</u> is not as obvious an endeavor as it may seem. Many of us have had people in our lives trying desperately (however good-intentioned) to encourage us to take certain directions—such as in our careers and relationships.

However, while these friends, parents, siblings, teachers, etc, may have our very best interests in mind, their choices are not necessarily the best and what is 'right' for us (that means FOR YOU). Only YOU can know precisely what is right for you—but that does not mean that you will simply 'know' right away.

For a moment, think back to your childhood. How many times did you change the end of the following sentence: *"when I grow up, I want to be…"?* The odds are that the number is pretty high! And it does not end with childhood. It follows you all the way through adolescence, and may still be with you today. Are you *sure* that you are on the exact path in your life that is BEST for you? One that will make YOU the happiest?

If your answer was "yes", then you are a rare individual indeed. If your answer was "no" however, you are far from alone! The majority of us, still have doubts and insecurities about different parts of our lives. What makes it even more frustrating, is that often when we feel that we are closest to figuring it all out, it turns out that nothing happens!

So, are we in fact doomed to just sit around and hope that fate sends us in the right direction? Of course not. It is time to start getting to know *you*, so that you too can understand what is best for you, and what choices you should make.

Getting to know yourself can take a good deal of *patience, determination, time, and concentration.* However, if you are to truly find your path and your happiness in life, it is vital that you take yourself through this process of *self-discovery.*

You will learn a great deal about yourself that you have MOST likely NEVER realized before, nor could you have put it into a coherent thought, let alone act on it. On this venture, you will discover your:

- Values

- Areas of interest

- Abilities

- Priorities

- Goals

- Strengths

- Weaknesses

- Thought process

This is a very important step, because BEFORE you can possibly take advantage of what the world has to offer you, you must (i) first understand yourself, (ii) your desires, and (iii) what you are able to accomplish. You need to look inside yourself and focus on *you*. (iv) What are *your* needs? (v) What is the future *you* want—not the one your friends and family want for you?

Of course, as wonderful as you are about to discover that you are, you will also most likely find that you have BOTH strengths <u>and</u> weaknesses. These make a big difference in the decisions that you can make and what will make you happy in life. Take a good and long look at everything that you have to offer. This can include your skills, natural talents, and the situations where you truly shine.

Even the smallest abilities that may seem insignificant can become something very important to your life (and impacting the lives of others) **Remember: Most big ideas start with something really small and then grow to become truly special. Pen and paper in hand, take a look deep inside yourself and make a list of all of those great things that make you who you are.**

You will also want to discover your *personality type*. This will play a large role in the paths that you will be able to successfully take in your life concerning your personal life, your relationships, your career, and all of the other important aspects of your life.

Naturally, we all have our own personalities, however, as unique as you may be, the odds are that your personality falls into a certain type, which can help you determine what you will enjoy doing the most.

- Are you an extrovert who is outgoing, loves being around people, and prefers leadership?

- Are you an introvert who prefers to remain more quiet, keeping only a few close friends, and preferring to work behind the scenes than in the spotlight?

Answering these types of questions, will increase your chances of making the right life choices. However, there is no reason for you to rush to find the answer. These answers will only come to you when you take the time to truly search your inward self.

So, how exactly do you take a good look at yourself and get to know yourself? Good question; and the answers lie in **seven important steps**.

Before we get to the steps, I wanted to look at the lives of women that I think are doing a really great job in life; not only are they living the American dream, but they also serve as "role models" for us. With that being said, let me also make it clear that we all make mistakes and celebrities are no different. However, in some way, each of these women that I have written about has been able to come back from controversy and lead happy, fulfilled lives. Take a closer look at another one.

GREAT EXAMPLE: BETHANY HAMILTON

Born into a family of surfing fanatics, on the Hawaii coastline and surf-prone enticing waves, off the island of Kauai, Bethany met her match, in the water, that changed her life, in an instant. As her instant love for surfing grew since being placed on a surfboard for the first time as a young toddler, coming to faith in Jesus Christ at age 5, winning professional surfing competitions year-on-year (8-13 years old). Amateur and accomplished surfer, open women's 2nd place finish in NSSA National Championships, the road to professional surfing started calling with much promise. But a life-challenging encounter with a shark changed all that, seemingly and at first!

On October 31, 2003 while surfing, a 14 ft. Tiger Shark attacked with a vengeance and severed her left arm, while she was lying flat on her board. Her blood loss was severe (60% by the time she got to shore) and friends and family came to her rescue and are recognized for stopping the bleeding and saving her life.

Her positive attitude is an epitome of the saying "an attitude of gratitude gives you altitude"! It is also what saved her life, then and now. With numerous surgeries, no infections and healing well underway, she is an inspiration to many to keep going, dig deeper, and reach higher! She remains determined to make her dreams come true, keep going, living her life. She is no longer merely the shark-attack, teenage victim. She never knew if she would be able to surf again, but she hit the water less than a month after the incident and encounter with the shark, with tenacity and determination.

Surfing with one arm proved to be no real challenge for this youngster that just kept going! Soon, she was back on track (returning to competition in early 2004 already). She does not expect or demand attention or special treatment. Quite the contrary, she wants equal change for everyone and no preferential compromises made for her. She does not want sympathy or empathy, she just wants to surf, compete and enjoy her life—even in the water!

She won 1st place in 2005 at the NSSA National Championships (Explorer Women's Division), her 1st national title surfing! Other accomplishments on this young lady's impressive track record includes: 3rd place (6-star ASP WQS), 2008 Roxy Pro Women's Surf Festival. She is surfing and competing at the highest levels, happy to be just another competitor without the fuss and attention her notoriety gets her.

Her public life and profile personality keeps her busy, as well as charitable work, speaking engagements, telling her story and inspiring others is also very important to her. Her slogan: Me quit? NEVER! She continues to encourage and inspire peers and others all around the world, who hear about her story of survival and tenacity, rebound and courage, against amazing odds. She is part of the Beating the Odds Foundation and World Vision International, with many TV and in-print appearances. She is focused on the real meaning of what she has to say, not just the story of what happened to her. The real significance of the message of her experience, life, choices!

While some might characterize her as the best-come-back athlete, she wants to be known for something a little different and in addition to that and special courage awards. Her biography Soul Surfer (released in October 2004), inspired a motion picture (2008). Devotional books and other Christian inspirational writings from her pen keep coming, DVD-release in 2009 of Heart of Soul Surfer, a documentary, shows how Bethany does not want to have the focus and attention all to herself.

Quite the contrary, she has humility and does not think of herself with an inflated ego, even if getting back in the water was not altogether that easy! Even when swimming, living and surfing with a prosthetic arm. She keeps making the most of her life, circumstances and keeps sharing her positive outlook on life, with everyone interested and who wants to listen and experience it for themselves!

In her own words: *"I can't change it, That was God's plan for my life and I'm going to go with it."*

THE SEVEN STEPS
TO KNOWING YOURSELF

Self-awareness is not something that you can just discover right away, but is, instead, a process that usually takes *seven important steps*. These steps are not actually as defined as they may seem at first. Instead, they may be taken out of sequence, and you will likely discover that they will often overlap, as you progress along the path to *self-discovery*.

Keep in mind, that no matter who we are, we are all _works-in-progress_. Though these seven steps will help to get you started along the right path for knowing yourself, **self-discovery is a process that lasts a lifetime.**

Step 1: Spend Some Quality Time With Yourself Every Day

"You never find yourself until you face the truth."

—Pearl Bailey

To get to know yourself then, you need to spend some good quality time with just you. True, we all have busy lives, and it isn't always easy to find time for yourself, but consider it something you cannot afford _not_ to do. Everyone needs to _make_ the time to be alone, with pen-in-hand, _(making a list of everything that you know you want in life)._

Back when I was in high school, I knew that I wanted to be a model. However, I was also aware that there were several things that I would require in order to make that dream into a reality. So, I did just what you are going to undertake and do now _(and what I still do today)!_ I wrote down a list of all the things that I would need in order to become a model.

Not only does this process allow you to identify the different stages that you would need to pass before you can reach your goal, but it will also allow you to look deep inside yourself, to find out _where you are spending your time_, _how you are spending it_, and _with whom you are spending it._

Recognizing your own behavior patterns is an important part of getting to know yourself. Just as important, however, is observing the types of people in your life. People have a tremendous influence on your path, and can either help to build you up along the way, or can tear you down, keeping you from your greater potential and dreams realization.

Something I have always realized is that the quality of life that you wish to live depends heavily on the people who are in your life at the time. Look around and consider your friends, as well as all the other people you choose to be around.

- Are these people who take a positive outlook on life and who are always there to support you?

- Are they people with a negative attitude, who would rather complain about their lives than take action to change?

- Do your friends share and respect your dreams, helping you to develop them, and build you up when you are feeling low?

- Do your friends make you doubt the decisions you have made, and make you feel guilty about your life choices?

As you get to know yourself, it is important that you learn to listen to your inner-voice, or intuition (as it is often called). I have been using and listening to my own inner-voice for the larger part of my life, by visualizing what I want out of life.

Most people would call this daydreaming or a total waste of time, but I would challenge that yet again. Do not judge a book by its cover! Just because it does not look like you are getting anything done, does not mean that the activity does not have any value. It is a powerful tool; as long as you use it in the right place and time, appropriately. Your *inner-voice* can help you <u>clarify the image of the life that you want to live</u>, and <u>what you will need to do to get there</u>.

It is important that while you listen to your inner-voice, you never second-guess it. I never do, because I understand that it is there in order to guide me. If you choose NOT to listen to your inner-voice, it may be because you simply do not *want* to hear, or fear what it has to say, and that alone does not mean or justify. that you *shouldn't*!

SIDEBAR: For example, in my own experience when I was in my early twenties, I had a friend who was not good for me. I made many excuses for her behavior, certain that I would be able to help her. It was quite a while before I allowed myself to realize that she was not a true friend to me, and she was not equally concerned about what was best for me. It was not a two-way street or reciprocal, balanced, positive mutually-beneficial relationship. It was quite one-sided actually.

It took a great deal of strength to make the decision to remove her from my life entirely. Even more difficult to take the necessary actions that I needed to follow to indeed get her out of my life. If I had listened to my inner-voice all along, it would not have come to that point. My inner-voice told me that she was not a good person for me to be around. But, I had to learn this lesson personally, the hard way, as many people do.

I want to be clear that this can be very difficult. Make no mistake about it! When you decide to eliminate somebody from your life, it is not easy and you will feel a lot of different emotions. This is normal.

However, if you find that you have several people in your life like this, do not attempt to make the whole shift all at once, because it can be very emotionally draining. Start out by limiting phone calls and your association with these people. Little by little, it will become easier for you. You may need to change your email address, in addition to a new home and cell phone number. It may sound extreme, but in most cases, this is the easiest way not to have to hear from them again.

You will start to see that this is the right decision and you might very well be able to witness the growing positive changes, due to your ability to release them. You will even begin making new friends that are healthier influences and companions for you. I know now, that I have the most incredible group of friends anyone can wish for. People that I care about deeply, and who want the best for each other, while being there for one another, in a positive, uplifting way. Having friends like that in your life is such a blessing!

We have been given this inner guide as a compass, and by learning to get to know ourselves, we can learn to use that compass, and behave accordingly. Use your compass to take a full account of who you are, and who is in your life. Then, decide right away whether or not each of these people is good for you, or not!

By learning to listen to myself and trust what my inner voice was saying, I started naturally attracting the right kind of friends for me. These are people who truly care about my happiness and support me in my dreams and my goals.

This can include anybody with whom you choose to spend your own time. It may be a friend, boyfriend, family member, or other person that you have some boundaries and sense of shared control, give-and-take. It may seem difficult at first, but you need to weed out the negative people in your life in order to enable yourself to move forward, follow your inner voice, and achieve your dreams and your goals.

Keeping a positive attitude must not only be something that you do to your surroundings, but it must be something that you bring into yourself. Through this effort, you should arise each morning with a smile in your heart. If this is difficult at first, then reassure yourself by saying these words out loud:

"This is going to be a great day, and something wonderful is going to happen to me."

SIDEBAR: I personally say this phrase every morning with my husband, so that we can affirm together that the day will be great, even before we have rolled out of bed. It helps me to start in a positive frame of mind, and start the day off right. By beginning every day by focusing on how wonderful it will be, you will find that you are much better prepared to handle anything that comes your way.

Your next step is to recognize that you will always have more to learn about yourself, and there will always be ways for you to improve your life. Therefore, some of the time that you spend with yourself should include reading a chapter out of a book *(such as this one!)*, so that you will continually remind yourself to grow and learn new things.

Consider yourself a student of your own life. As a student, you can never stop learning, because without learning, you will cease to grow.

As a part of your "studies", you should write your goals down on paper, focusing on them. Visualize yourself living the life that you have always wanted to live. This may include obtaining the ideal job, or moving into your dream home. It could be a perfect wedding with Prince Charming, or raising a healthy, well-balanced child and a happy family life.

Whatever your goals, you need to realize and occasionally remind yourself that everything you want in life can be yours, *as long as you take the right action steps to get there.*

Think deeply about your life, where you are in it, where you are headed, and how you will get there.

To get yourself started, consider the following questions:

- Do I spend each day working toward my dreams and goals, or am I wasting my time by simply "getting by" every day?

- With whom am I associating today who is positive?

- Who is a negative influence that I will need to break away from, in order to be able to move forward?

- Which people in my life are helping me grow?

- Which people, groups or individuals, are hindering me?

- What bad habits have I allowed to slip into my daily life that I need to put a stop to?

- Which new habits can I add to my life that will be positive for me and bring me joy?

- What positive risks should I take to ensure better self-integrity, a more "true me", or better intimacy with those people who are important to me?

- Is there a person in my life toward whom I am holding resentment or anger, and who I need to forgive, so that I may release myself from these bonds and therefore grow and flourish?

Naturally, there are many more questions that you can ask yourself, but these should give you a good jumping-off point and conversation-starter!

Step 2: Write in a Journal Every Day

"Confront the dark parts of yourself, and work to banish them with illumination and forgiveness. Your willingness to wrestle with your demons will cause your angels to sing. Use the pain as fuel, as a reminder of your strength."

—August Wilson

Head out to the business supply store or stationary store at your next opportunity, and pick up a journal or notebook—not a diary, planner or scheduler. There is a difference between these types of tools.

- A diary is laid out in a way that you will use it to report different events as if you were writing it to someone else. *(In fact, if someone else was to read it, it would be linear enough to make sense to them).*

- On the other hand, a journal is a notebook that allows you to write down your thoughts, feelings, and reactions to things that happened to you. It might include certain insights you have had or discoveries made, as well as lists of things that you want, need, value, and wish to include among your goals.

You can also write about dreams—both those you dream during sleep-time, and those you daydream while you are awake—express your feelings, and allow yourself to use your intuition to its fullest. *(Your journal will be the perfect place for you to take down your guiding beliefs, thoughts, and action patterns, the things that get you stuck, and the new things you've developed).*

You can even use your journal to write letters to people who have hurt you—which you will never mail—even if it happened quite some time ago. When you have gone through an emotional trauma, time has no meaning, and you can get stuck in that feeling. By writing out the feelings of *frustration, anger, pain, sadness, and hurt* that you are feeling, you are in fact helping to bring yourself out of the trauma, time and hurtful event, feeling and past, into the present and the here- and-now, the new, where you can understand the situation with new clarity and interpretations.

This is one of the most effective ways to become aware of yourself, and integrate your experiences into recognition of who you are and who you are capable of being. It will not be long into your journal writing, that you discover that there are certain patterns in your life that repeat. This can include different thoughts, behaviors and revelations *(some that may even occasionally remind you of your parents and other important people in your life).*

By writing things out in a journal, you will become much more aware of beliefs and patterns that had previously been hidden, even though they were still impacting you on an unconscious level. By writing them out, they become visible to you and allow you to deal with them and heal yourself.

SIDEBAR: So many years of my own life have been spent writing in a journal. I have a great number of memories and experiences that are all recorded within the pages of simple notebooks, that allow me to look back and reflect on my life. These times have truly helped to transform me.

Writing in a journal may seem like a very simple step to take, but it is also a very important one. I usually write about everything happening in my life. This includes tough times, such as when there is a shake-up in a friendship, and better times, when I have felt very inspired. There aren't any rules to what I write in my journal. Essentially, I include anything and everything.

Not only do I find journals helpful when I'm writing them, but I can also look back at what I have written down to see how much I have grown. This really helps to keep me on track with my goals and my own personal growth.

I also find amazing the sheer number of things that seemed so important at the time (important enough that I wrote them down), and now they actually do seem quite funny—I have been able to move on, and can see the humor in my own behavior. After all, journals are not written for others to read, so they do not need to make sense to anybody but you/me. Just make sure that you keep your journal in a safe place that will be well away from any tempted, curious hands or eyes, in your home.

Give yourself sufficient amounts or allocations of your precious time every day to dedicate to your journal. Usually, twenty to thirty minutes is good enough every day. It may sound like a significant time-commitment at first if you have never written in a journal before, but if you try it for a month, you will soon find that this is a perfectly natural length of time for getting things down on paper.

Remember that since you are the only one who will ever see your journal, and that since you may or may not ever even read it again, you should not worry about completing sentences, using neat writing, and being accurate with your spelling or grammar. **All you need to do is express yourself. Just get it all down and in front of yourself. That is really the key!**

You will find this extremely helpful and a rest-haven in times of great change, stress, growth, healing, as well as holidays, anniversaries, painful events, or when you are feeling upset with someone else.

Journal writing is a process, *not just one step in seven*, for getting to know yourself.

One day may not bring you much self-discovery, but when you continue writing every day, over time you will discover a great deal of enrichment and comfort.

You will see the bigger picture—*patterns, themes, and details* you may not have even known were there.

Step 3: Identify Your Support System

"I am afraid to show you who I really am, because if I show you who I really am, you might not like it—and that's all I got."

—Sabrina Ward Harrison

Your next step is to discover the counselors, religious representatives, guides, teachers, helpers, and mentors, who can help you along the way, on your journey.

Though it is important to a degree, to be *independent, self-sufficient, and autonomous,* this does not mean that we can NEVER seek out others for support in our lives. If you are unable to look outside of yourself, then you will only struggle for your entire life.

True, there is value in being able to do things yourself, but we are social animals, and depend on the contribution of others for some levels of our fulfillment.

Unfortunately, it is not always easy to admit to other people that we are having problems and that we are having trouble healing. As much as emotional support can help us to heal faster, it can be very challenging discovering and trusting people with whom we can let go of control and admit that we need help.

Mentors, teachers, and therapists are all wonderful people for supporting you through times of trial, uncertainty and instability. Our lives can be very confusing and difficult to get through, but the guidance and support of those we can trust can be very beneficial.

Step 4: Learn from the People Around You

"A man should first direct himself in the way he should go. Only then should he instruct others."

—Buddha

We learn the most about ourselves when we learn about the people around us. In this sense, when you are trying to discover who you are, where you are headed in life, and how you are going to get there, one of the steps that you will need to take is to consider what you can learn from the people you spend time with.

Consider all of the people you know, including friends, family, acquaintances, co-workers, and all of the other people you have gotten to know throughout your life. *Write down this list so that you can use it for reference.* Then, think about each person individually, and consider what you have already learned, and still can learn from each of these people.

Consider their strengths, weaknesses, their motivations, and the decisions that they have made for their own lives. You can learn from both the positive and the negative in people. This means that you can not only improve yourself by learning from a strong quality that someone has, but you can also improve yourself by learning from mistakes and other negative things that people have done and that you do not want to repeat.

In my own life, I remember watching people from a young age, and deciding that for myself, I will live a "charmed life". To this end, I kept track of all of the people around me, looking into the things that they did which were positive and negative, so that I could emulate the positive, and avoid the negative. Modeling and mirroring became a very important part of my own path to self-discovery, and personal growth.

This doesn't mean that you should copy any specific person and try to become someone that you clearly are not. What it does mean, is that you can learn from what is happening around you; from the example that other people are setting.

This way, instead of simply walking blindly through life, thinking only about looking inside to learn about yourself, you will open your eyes and discover what others are doing. You will be more open to how it might/can make your life better, easier, more appealing, or bring you closer to your own goals.

People are all around you, doing their own thing. They live their lives, make their choices, and develop their own characters. Use these examples to help you build the "YOU" that you would like to be, and to achieve the goals that you want to reach.

Step 5: Read and Listen

"Trust yourself. You know more than you think you do."

—Dr. Benjamin Spock

Investigate the specific issues, relationships, spiritual growth, and healing that affect you by reading books and listening to tapes and CD's by wise teachers and inspirational muses. You are fortunate in that you live in a time that is filled with information readily available to everyone.

Everywhere you look, there are self-help books, websites, workshops, and lectures that you can attend in-person, online, or that can be recorded and watched later. There are teachers out there who have researched and dealt with just about every imaginable problem and life issue that you can dream up!

No longer are we isolated from or kept at bay, from information-sharing and resources that can help us to improve our lives, no matter where we live, from right across the country and globe.

Take your *self-knowledge* a step further and invest in your own individuality. Once you recognize the issues you face, get to know as much about them as you possibly can, so that you can make the best choices for you.

> **SIDEBAR:** This is precisely what I did. I made the decision to read all of the different materials that I could get my hands on. I am well aware of the potential that knowledge brings through the power of information. Opportunities become apparent only when we know what to look for.

I always have three or four different helpful books on the go at any given time. I feel that it gives me an edge in handling different situations—both positive and negative—that I need to face every day. Knowledge is extremely important. The more you learn about yourself, your life, and the way that you function, the better prepared you will be for making decisions—regardless of how important and/or seemingly insignificant—throughout your life.

Information is all around us and all we need to do is want to receive it. We have to consider if we want to take advantage of what it has to offer. Keep in mind that everything in life that is worth having is also worth the hard work that it will take to obtain it.

Learning is a part of this work, and every effort that you put forth to learn will take you another step closer to getting what you want from your life.

Step 6: Take Positive Risks

"Explore thyself. Herein are demanded the eye and the nerve."

—Henry David Thoreau

Once you have gathered information about yourself and how to deal with your specific issues, take the chance to talk about yourself and your problems with others. You have already been expressing yourself with your journal, looking into your goals, dreams, values, insights, etc, and now the time has come to take this awareness to a new level!

This step often takes a great deal of courage. Recognizing yourself on your own is still relatively safe, but without putting your ideas into practice, and offering them to others to get a new perspective and make them work for you, you will not be able to *use* all of your discoveries and self-revelation insights.

Each of your new choices will help you to better learn what works for you, and what does not. It is therefore time to take a few positive risks to allow yourself to continue moving forward.

You will know that you are ready to start taking these positive risks when you find yourself locating websites or buying books at a greater rate than you can actually read and process them!

It is important to learn to step outside of your own comfort zone. It is a part of the growing process, allowing you to learn and develop by leaps-and-bounds every time.

SIDEBAR: I am personally quite uncomfortable speaking in front of large groups of people. My preference is to speak in front of a camera. However, this fact does not stop me from speaking to groups quite frequently. I know that every time I head up there to speak, I come just a little bit closer to overcoming my fears. Otherwise, I would simply be letting those fears rob me of valuable experiences.

Taking risks is a critical part of life. However, there are risks that should be taken, and risks that would be wiser to avoid. Listen to your inner-voice to know which risks are right for you in your life.

Step 7: Enjoy Knowing Yourself

"Resolve to find thyself; and to know that he who finds himself, loses his misery."

—Matthew Arnold

Oddly enough, as noble a pursuit as *self-knowledge* may be, there is still a tendency amongst us all to feel guilty when we begin understanding ourselves to the degree that we can take our lives in a positive-change or improvement type direction. This is the time when you are actually able to consciously create your life, so that you achieve the results that you want.

This often brings about comments from others such as "you are so lucky," and "things always work out for you". Since you have not exactly been advertising your efforts toward self-knowledge, it may indeed look as though luck has suddenly been smiling on you. However, you will know that you have made a very large change in your life that has meant that you are more prepared to achieve what is right for you.

People will see what you have and want it without having to do the work that you have done to get there. Do not allow these people to stop you from enjoying your *self-knowledge*, and what you have achieved through its discovery.

Instead, spend time with those people who love and support the new growth so hard-earned!

> **SIDEBAR:** I have said it many times before, and I will say it again: Women simply do not give themselves enough of the credit that they deserve for everything that they do, accomplish, work towards, and achieve. Realize that you need to let yourself off-the-hook sometimes, and never forget to applaud your own accomplishments.

This is very important, and will allow your self-esteem to flourish. With good self-esteem, you will get to know yourself even better, and ensure that you are becoming the best "you" that you can be.

Get Started With Your Own Personality Quiz

Now that you know what steps you will need to take in order to find yourself, you may be ready to get going. However, you need to remind yourself that this is still a process, and not something that will bring results to you instantly or by tomorrow. It does not quite work like that!

To get you started and motivated for these seven steps, use the following quiz to begin understanding your general personality type. This will NOT allow you to get to know your true, unique self, but it will give you an overall idea of who you are, and where you may wish to begin the investigation into yourself.

Write down your answers in the spaces provided so that you do not forget your answers BEFORE you can find out your results.

Remember that this quiz has no right or wrong answers. Follow your feelings to answer honestly, and find out about some of your true natures.

Question 1

Your schedule is completely free tonight, and your closest friends call you to suggest a bowling night. Do you:

☐ Boot up your computer to create the most logical carpool route, then create the order by which everyone will take their turn.

☐ Say "Great!" and then begin bragging about how great your bowling skills are—even if they are not so great.

☐ Laugh, then phone, email, and talk to everyone you know, to tell them that you and your friends are going bowling.

☐ Take this as the ideal opportunity for getting to know that guy in the group that you have been drooling over for a while now.

☐ Roll your eyes and inform your friends that you do not like bowling and that they can go without you.

Question 2

It's your birthday. What do you hope to receive?

☐ A beautiful leather jacket.

☐ An enormous birthday cake, with ice cream to go with it. The movie and matching collector figurines are a bonus.

☐ You do not ever expect anything for your birthday, but a book or something like that would be lovely.

☐ A cute stuffed animal.

☐ A night out with the man you love.

Question 3

You have had a long day, and you are just about to flop down on the couch for the evening, but you need to choose a snack first. You:

- ☐ Make a pot of tea, and put a handful of cookies on a plate.

- ☐ Grab a family-sized bag of chips, and a bottle of soda.

- ☐ Pour a glass of water, and enjoy some whole-wheat crackers and a sprig of grapes.

- ☐ Mix it up with a few cookies, some chips, cheese puffs, and some fruit juice.

- ☐ Choose whatever is there. It doesn't matter what.

Question 4

Consider your own view on Happiness. Is it:

- ☐ Never indulge too much, or the fall will be too hard when it is over.

- ☐ Real happiness must be shared.

- ☐ It is what we all should live for.

- ☐ It comes and goes with the snap of your fingers

- ☐ It is something that we never truly appreciate until we lose it.

Question 5

You have decided to go to the movies. What kind of movie are you most likely to choose?

- ☐ A good comedy.

- ☐ You never go to the movies.

- ☐ A really mushy romance.

- ☐ A documentary about a female leader's struggle to rise to power.

- ☐ A thriller that is simply action-packed.

Question 6
What do you enjoy most when you come home from work?

- ☐ Heading out to a restaurant with your closest friends and/or family members.

- ☐ Taking part in sports such as soccer, tennis, basketball or whatever sport you enjoy the most.

- ☐ Curling up on the sofa with a bag of cookies and a "chick flick".

- ☐ Catching up on your sleep.

- ☐ Reading a good thick book.

Question 7
What do you think of horoscopes, palm readers, fortunetellers, and tarot cards?

- ☐ They are fun to do, but should not be taken too seriously.

- ☐ A silly waste of time.

- ☐ Effective ways to prepare for what is coming. You read your daily horoscope, and your psychic knows you by name without even using her psychic abilities.

- ☐ A rip-off. It is just people who are trying to get your money.

- ☐ You hold your own séances with your friends.

Question 8

You are responsible for a seminar in front of all of your most important clients. Do you:

☐ Think about it the first night you get it, and then forget about it until the last minute when you whip something together.

☐ Create an enormous presentation including PowerPoint®, pamphlets, handouts, and guest speakers.

☐ List the main ideas of your research, and then just let the moment take you when you are up in front of the group.

☐ Hold an interactive discussion with baked goods, coffee, tea, and imported water to give it that extra "oomph".

☐ Gather a good deal of great information and then set it all into a basic presentation whose content speaks for itself.

Question 9

On any given day, your home is:

☐ A disaster area. It is practically a fire hazard with all of the clutter strewn about.

☐ Perfectly neat. It has matching furniture with personal touches to finish it off. They could photograph it for a magazine.

☐ Relatively empty. The bare necessities are there, but there is nothing on the walls, and little else to make it warm or cozy.

☐ All about you. Sure, it is probably not what a professional decorator would want, but every bit of your place means something to you, and represents your own taste.

☐ White walls, white furniture, few wall decorations. It is relatively neutral, and you do not really prioritize decorating.

Question 10
With one million dollars, you would:

☐ Spend it all right away.

☐ Give yourself a shopping spree, but save the rest.

☐ Invest it all.

☐ Buy what you truly need, and then save what is left.

☐ Buy something great for someone you really care about, and then hide the rest.

Answer Key

Go over your answers and circle the corresponding numbers in the table below:

	Answer (a)	(b)	(c)	(d)	(e)
Question 1	5	4	3	2	1
Question 2	1	3	5	2	4
Question 3	2	4	5	3	1
Question 4	1	4	3	2	5
Question 5	3	1	2	5	4
Question 6	4	3	2	1	5
Question 7	5	1	4	3	2
Question 8	4	5	3	2	1
Question 9	2	5	3	4	1
Question 10	3	2	5	1	4

Now add up the number of times your answer received a 1, 2, 3, 4, or 5

# of 1's	# of 2's	# of 3's	# of 4's	# of 5's

In which group did you score the highest?

Group 5

If the majority of your answers scored a "5", then you are likely a very self-motivated individual who strives very hard to do your best at everything that you do. You may not be a workaholic, but you may have some of those tendencies. You likely prefer to have one or two very close friends to having a large group of friends who are not as tight. You take your time when you are doing things to ensure that they have been done properly.

Group 4

If you scored a "4" on most of your answers, then you are most likely a freethinker. You are quite the individual who does not follow what other people do as an example of how to behave and act. Some may consider you silly, but you just do not take life too seriously, that is all. You are generous and you are fun to be around. You may, however, have trouble realizing what a great person you truly are.

Group 3

If most of your answers were "3"s then you are likely a person who just loves to live. You like everything that life has to offer. Though you may get down in the dumps every now and again, it is not very often, and it does not last very long. You are energetic and fun loving. You attract many people, and folks tend to want to be like you. Many people lose your flair for life as they go through puberty. It takes a special person to hang in there.

Group 2

If your score is mostly "2"s, then you are a friendly, kind, and quirky individual. You like to have fun, and you want everyone to join in when you do. You are always looking for fun and exciting ways to let loose and to express yourself, and you are always looking for new people to do this with.

Group 1

If you have scored primarily "1"s, then you enjoy life when it is simple and low key. You are by no means boring, but you do enjoy sensibility and stability in your life. You enjoy being around other people, but you would be just as happy not drawing attention to yourself. You can work well both alone, and in small groups, but you would rather have tasks delegated to each individual, than actually work on the same item with another person. You are very autonomous.

WHAT YOU SHOULD LEARN FROM THIS CHAPTER

Key-reminders and insights from Chapter 3, highlight:

- To achieve happiness and success in your life, it is vital that you first get to know yourself. Then, you will be able to discover what you want, what you are able to achieve, and how you can get there.

- Getting to know yourself is a process, not something that you can simply discover overnight. Take a good look at yourself and use the 7 steps in this chapter to achieve self-knowledge.

- Listen to your inner voice, and never second-guess what it has to say. Consider it your life's compass.

- Ask yourself questions, starting with broad, general ones, and narrowing them down to very specific issues in your life. Take the time to find the honest and true answers.

- Learn the power of the pen and paper, and write down your thoughts, feelings, impressions, and inspirations. You'll be amazed at the difference you'll find simply be putting your day or your goals into words.

- Realize that even if this is a journey to self-discovery, you cannot isolate yourself from the world and live without help and support.

Chapter 4

The Decisions You Make Today Will Create Your Tomorrow. Choose Wisely

"Nothing is more difficult, and therefore more precious, than to be able to decide."

—*Napoleon Bonaparte*

D ecisions, even seemingly insignificant ones, can have a staggeringly large impact on the future and the rest of our lives. This is why it is so important to make our choices with care today, to ensure that we have set ourselves up for the right tomorrow.

When you make decisions, you rely very heavily on your past experiences to guide you, going through a full process of different thoughts and influences. There are, however, a number of rules that you can follow, to help guide you along the right path to making better quality decisions.

There are two primary things that you should know about good decision-making, right off the bat.

Good decisions come from disciplined thinking. If you follow the basic laws of decision-making, most of your plans will work out. Thinking haphazardly when you make a decision, little of what you plan will actually pan out. Thinking is the key word here. I spend at least an hour every day in quiet time, reviewing my life goals and where I currently stand.

There are always decisions that need to be made, and I want to make sure that I make the right choice for my life. The only way to do this is to make my life restful, tranquil and 'silently welcoming'. This includes turning off the computer, any cell phones, and TV, spending quality time alone, thinking and pondering every situation that comes up. This is also very relaxing and you will find it incredibly valuable in your daily life. *(I know that you will savor your time alone and start enjoying it more, the more you take time to stick to it!)*.

Forming good habits makes the right decisions automatic. Form a good habit today. Each time you make the right decision, you gain the necessary self-confidence to keep making good decisions. That is why following the laws of decision-making is crucial.

Therefore, if you set certain rules for yourself, disciplining your thoughts for making good decisions, and then create a habit of it, you will perpetually improve your decision-making process, and make good decisions much more frequently.

Put differently, this does not mean that you will not make any mistakes, BUT that you WILL find that...

(i) You at least make better choices than the worst-case scenario!

(ii) The most important decisions you are making for your life are the right ones.

(iii) The wrong choices are hopefully smaller and less significant in the overall scheme of your life. *By creating this new habit of disciplined thinking, you will see that it becomes easier every time you need to make a decision.*

A GREAT EXAMPLE: HILARY SWANK

We do not all make perfect decisions for ourselves, but it is important to keep on top of what we want. This is to ensure that the decisions that we are making, and the decisions that we have made in the past, continue to work their magic for us.

Hilary Ann Swank has a great life-story to both share and inspire, especially those getting a rough start in their lives, with the odds stacked against them!

She is a wonderful example of someone who has made the type of decisions that have worked well for her, serving her dreams positively, a helping at a time, throughout her life.

Learning from an early age, that small steps, overcoming mistakes and pulling through, beating the odds so to speak, matter, and can make a difference. There is much to be learned from this inspirational gal. This is especially true, when she goes about her life and business, with elegance, personal gusto, commitment, style and grace!

Born on 30 July 1974, in Bellingham, Washington, USA this young child-star debutant, is recognized as the third youngest woman in history to win two Academy Awards for "Best Performance by an Actress in a Leading Role". Film critics adore this damsel, landing her many supporting roles, also ones starring across from headliners like Clint Eastwood, Morgan Freeman, and many others.

Even through and following her divorce, she stays positive and herself, delving deep in the face of turmoil and trouble! A marriage -break-up following an 8+

year-long journey together with her husband and love of her life, saw that road end for Hilary and Chad Lowe.

Despite some personal set-backs and challenges, she was also the top-pick of the popular vote for "People" magazine's 50 Most Beautiful People in 2000, 2004 and 2005. She is admired for many reasons, but among her claims to fame, is that she had been a successful professional actress since the age of 16. To this day, she still improvises and immerses herself totally in her roles and work, going beyond the call of duty (for example, shaving her head, hair, even dressing up like a boy for a month (even when going out in public) for a role, or getting bulked up, gaining weight, training professionally to be optimally, physically fit, to play a champion-boxer, convincingly).

She is an all-rounder all-star athlete, sporting great wins and championships in swimming and gymnastics. Today, her life is a far cry from these belied humble beginnings, where being in a strange place, new city, with her mother (Judy Swank), impoverished, struggling to make ends meet and living from their car, on the streets, to earning millions of dollars, walking the red carpet with confidence and poise, never looking back.

Bulking up to be the first woman to win an Oscar for portraying a boxer, securing two nominations <u>and</u> two wins (joining the ranks of Vivien Leigh, Helen Hayes, Sally Field and Luise Rainer, sets her in a class of her very own!

Decisions to get somewhere and be somebody early in life, believing in her dream, working to make it happen, finally got rewarded with a lucrative career.

It meant that taking the right route *(out of the trailer park, as she so oftentimes reminds others!).* For her, it meant a hard-working road with a plan, instead of the easy way out, or *proverbial road paved with gold* where others made it happen for you. Today, she sports a star on the Hollywood walk of fame (# 2,325!), to top it all off!

There are many things in life that can be or seem emotionally and physically overwhelming. However, time and again she shines! Hilary takes a fresh approach, inspires others, has very clear directions and sticks to making her plan work and living her dream life. Popular and appreciated, she keeps raking in new movie-deals and iconic on-screen parts. She debuted her film career in Buffy the vampire slayer, back in 1992 and has been going strong since.

Even when decisions are hard to make and seem extremely difficult, making them well and deliberately, have paid off for her. It can for you too! Remember: she has proven to be a success and did not allow what others were saying to hold her back. She is a gutsy lady and this is one reason why I love her!

In her own words, on being an actress…

"As in life, your mind can be the hugest obstacle or tool, depending on how you choose to use it. And I find that a lot of people who are successful in life say, "I can do this, and I will do this." Their minds don't get in their way; whereas people who wake up and say, "Oh, I can't," their mind is in their way, and it's going to stop them from doing what they need to do to achieve their dream."

SEVEN RULES FOR DECISION MAKING

The following are ***seven essential rules*** that you should implement to help yourself create great decision-making habits:

Focus on the most important thing—This seems obvious, but it is the decision-making principle that is most often violated. People overload the decision-making process with so many variables, that what is REALLY important oftentimes gets lost. It is important that you know the "WHY" in your life.

Why do you want this or that? What does it bring you? Understanding the reason behind it will keep you focused on the goal that is in front of you.

Example: Most decisions only require you to answer one yes or no question, such as, do I really like him? Do I want this job? Do we launch this product? But then someone says, "what about this?" And someone else says, "what about that?"

What should have been a straight-forward decision gets confused by minor considerations. You lose the focus required for making the right decision. If you know why you are doing something, the reason or rationale behind your goal, you WILL stay focused on getting there and the decisions that you make will hopefully also guide you to the shortest route for reaching your goal.

An illustrative, practical example would be completing college. Sure, you want to go and have fun, and yes I am sure it will make your parents proud to see you go to college, but the "why" for going should be reaching your academic or career goals. Of course, having fun and enjoying the journey is a part of it, but your "why" is that now you can become a teacher, a lawyer or enter whatever field you are interested in.

In every decision, one factor usually is the most important, above all. Close your eyes and concentrate on that element, forgetting all other considerations. Once you are focused only on what is most important, the odds are you will make the right decision. Everything else is a detail.

Turn big decisions into a series of little decisions—Some decisions appear overwhelming. You want to focus on what is most important, but there are so many unknowns, that your focus gets blurred. This is where that quiet time each day comes into play. You can write things out and really take the time to go over them and think them through.

Example: Taking a new job means learning new skills, moving to a new city and so on. With so many variables to juggle, you wind up making a bad decision—or no decision at all. Planning is the KEY to allowing the decisions that you make to come to full fruition. Once you know that you are making the right choices, you have to have a great plan to execute each step to reaching your goal.

**Break that big decision into several smaller,
more manageable decisions.**

Take time to study the new employer in depth. Decide if it is a company you really want to work for. Spend a few days in the new city. Decide if you want to live there. Are you single? Is it a safe area? Do you have young children and do you need to look into making sure they have good schools? Look into where you want to live… in short, ask many and key questions. Find out about the town online and see what it has to offer.

**After you make all the little decisions,
the big decision will essentially be made!**

Base your decision on self-acceptance—Self-acceptance covers a lot of ground…

- *What you like.*

- *What you are interested in.*

- *What you are good at.*

- *What you feel is best for you at this time in your life.*

Any decision based on <u>who you really are</u>—for example, how <u>you really work</u> and <u>what you really like</u>, probably will all work out and for the better.

Problem: People think a decision will transform them from who they are to who they would like to be. Job offers are NOT measured by suitability—as they should be—but by whether they will make them better people. Their future becomes hostage to that lack of *self-acceptance.* A decision made under such circumstances, may very well be a disaster waiting to happen!

Ask yourself what you really like and what makes you comfortable. If the decision will not add to your feeling of comfort, it probably would prove to be a bad decision. Listen to your inner-voice, as was discussed earlier in the book. What does your *gut* (your intuition) tell you about the circumstance? ***Chances are you already know the answer and you just have to decide to make the right choice.***

Consider all the good things your decision can bring—Decision-making is, for many people, an exercise in *disaster avoidance.*

Instead of making the decision that might cause something wonderful to happen, we often make the decision we hope will hurt us the least, or the path of least resistance, if you will.

We make emotional decisions based sometimes on what we would like to ideally happen, instead of what is actually good for us. For example, you are very attracted to a man, but he lives and works in your city, and you are moving to go to college, or because of a very attractive job offer. The right thing for you may very well be to simply remain friends with this man and allow yourself to pursue your education or career, while meeting other people along the way.

However, it is easy to be tempted to try a difficult long-distance relationship because of an emotional reason. This is not really what may be BEST for you, or in your own interest.

Reality check: There is absolutely nothing wrong with running through possible negative outcomes when making a decision. It would be foolish to make decisions on the assumption that nothing could go wrong. But decisions turn sour when you fail to examine positive scenarios as well. I play out every possible scenario in my mind to help me decide on what I should do. Again, I keep my goals in mind, and my "why"—this always seems to help me make sense of things. ***As many possibilities as possible MUST be examined to help ensure the right outcome!***

SIDEBAR: Let us say your friend asks you for a loan and you decide that you have the money to give to her and that you trust her to pay you back. You need to think about the fact that something may happen to make her unable to pay you back, when you may need that money. You need to consider that she may decide not to pay you back at all. In this case you must tell her *"Sure, I will lend you the money. However, we'll need to draw up a promissory note for you to sign. I do believe that you are good for the money, but my CPA has recommended it to me for tax purposes."* That is all you need to say. If she hesitates to sign it, then simply DO NOT lend her the money. Now you have saved yourself time, money, frustration, and in all likelihood, also your friendship!

However, after considering the negative outcomes, the decision-making process must be fueled by the possibility that your decision will lead to something wonderful—*a new career, a stronger relationship or marriage, etc.*

Keep reworking the decision, until you see it leading to something wonderful. If you rework the decision and nothing wonderful emerges, you risk making the wrong decision. It really *is* that simple!

Get what you need to make your decision a success—Especially in business, this rule gets broken again and again.

A meeting ends with the decision to do such-and-such, but no plans are made to implement the decision. Write it down and create an action strategy that follows. If others are involved, write out their names and responsibilities on paper. If you are in charge, then you need to make sure that they are getting it done. By writing it down, you have something to follow that will keep you on track and focused. *(I cannot stress this point enough!)*.

If there is no passion to implement the decision—OR if you know in advance that the resources you need will not be available—you have not decided anything. It is window dressing meant to satisfy someone's ego, or to be included in a report to show your department is on the ball!

Show up, discover your passion, and apply it in everything you take on. Projects at work or school may come and go, but if you can find your passion in each new project, you will love what you do. Others will also recognize your leadership and positive outlook. It will inspire them to want to do the same. Live with passion and DO NOT sit on the side-lines… NOT EVER!

Start with how you ARE going to
implement your decision and work backward.

Keep things as simple as possible—Even smart people break this law. Because they see the big picture, they want the decision to cover every issue that might arise. They draft plans so that no possibility is overlooked. Test this for yourself, you will see it to be true, just like I said earlier and suggest here! Examine BOTH *what can go right* and *what can go wrong*. Remember though, that simplicity is always best when making your action list.

Reality: The more things that can go wrong, the more things probably *will* go wrong. You will learn how to maneuver your way through obstacles and once you become good at getting out of a bad decision early-on, you will stop making poor choices that quickly.

Venture capitalists are justifiably wary of overly complicated plans for a new business. Business plans that are easy to grasp are the ones that are most likely to get funding. They want ideas that will attract the masses! It is hard enough to brand a new product without having to over-explain what it is about, or justify the reason for it.

Consider all your options—I have never met a decision maker—good or bad—who had checked out all possible options. Invariably, I come up with options never considered.

POSITIVE DECISION MAKING ATTITUDE

A positive attitude to life helps make major decision-making far easier and less stressful.

Here are some attitude changes that you need to make BEFORE you make a choice... *this may be regarding any decision that may have an impact on your future:*

- Get rid of your mental blocks.

- Give up the notion that there is only one 'right solution' to the problem/ dilemma you are confronting.

- Do not fear making a mistake.

- View your problems as a normal part of life.

- See yourself not as an indecisive person; but rather someone who "sometimes" behaves indecisively.

- Use your words to create your future. Speak positively over your life and your plans.

- Develop your intuition and logic, but listen to what your heart says (your gut feeling).

- Stop and think before you act. Stop yourself from doing the first thing you think of.

- Be specific.

Know what your goals and your values are, the principles of your existence, before making a major life decision. Ask yourself if the ideal outcome is in alignment with your values.

Write down all the positive and negative factors for and against taking a particular course of action. Benjamin Franklin did it in two columns when confronted with major decisions. *(Benjamin Franklin was one of our country's founding fathers, a skilled businessman, a scientist, an inventor, a statesman, philosopher, a musician, and the country's first millionaire. When Benjamin Franklin had a major decision to make, he would examine the situation and make a list of all the factors favoring each of his possible options. Then, based on all the information on his list, he would make his decision).*

- Think how the decision will benefit you first. Do what YOU and not what other people really want.

- Try to think calmly and rationally.

- Do your homework and get all the facts BEFORE you make the decision.

- Get opinions and feedback from others you trust, but DO NOT let them make the decision for you. If you like the lives they live, then chances are that they have made great decisions to get there.

- Model and mirror these "lifestyle mentors" in the positive disciplines that they have can be added to your life. Try them out and see if they work for you.

- Establish priorities and "soul-search" (for a "soul-mate"). Ask yourself what are the critical factors? What is the single most important consideration?

- Trust your impulses, your "gut-feelings". (DO NOT forget the inner-voice discussed in Chapter 2.) Make a decision based on what IS right for you, NOT an emotional decision that you know is wrong, but is easier or more appealing. All this usually does, is prolong the inevitable.

- When you make a decision, realize that it can take years to change the outcome. Here is an *example*: if you marry the wrong person, then that can take years to resolve. If you decide to have children with this person, then you have, in some ways, kept that person in your life indefinitely. These are two of the most critical decisions that you can make. Other decisions that have been made along the wrong path can be worked out more easily when they are not as important. Chances are that you can work your way through it and make the correction. But I have seen too many people that I know who have married the wrong person when they already knew deep inside that they should not have married that person in the first place. Their entire lives have to now be charted on a course they have and will come to regret.

- Do realize, however, that some mistakes will provide you with a learning experience that you most likely need. You will never do the right thing all the time. None of us do. So if you do make a mistake, take the opportunity to learn from it so you do not keep making the same one. Look for opportunities in any decision. Each "mistake" is an opportunity to learn. When you make mistakes, DO NOT beat yourself up over it. Just say to yourself: *"Well, I messed up! I will never do that again..."* and move on.

- Accept total responsibility for your decisions. Responsibility is not blame—so do not blame others for putting yourself in this predicament. This attitude helps to relieve your anger or resentment and gives one peace of mind. It is not always easy to accept responsibility, but this will help you grow and mature, and others will have respect for you because of it.

- Change course if your strategy is not working—the quality of your life is at stake. Learn when to correct your direction. Bear in mind that pilots are off-course on their flight-path 90% of the time because they are always making corrections to meet their final destination... When driving, you are also continually making little corrections. Pay attention. This way, you will be able to make corrections to mistakes as early into the error as possible.

- Be prepared to take a few risks in life. Look out for opportunities. Every successful business or venture started out with an idea which was a risk. Nothing is infallible. The knowledge that you can handle anything that comes your way is your key to allowing yourself to take risks. Security is a state of mind. It is not *having* things, it is *handling* things. Take a well thought out leap of faith.

- Look ahead to the future—the past is already gone. See the path ahead as an adventure into the unknown and a time for challenge.

Go for it! Live your life with GUSTO! Passion is contagious!

SELF CONFIDENCE

To succeed, you need self-confidence. Luckily, self-confidence is easy to obtain if you take the right steps. If you feel you lack self-confidence... have no fear! YOU CAN GROW IT!

Everyone has made bad decisions at some point in their lives: choosing friends who stab you in the back, saying the wrong thing to your spouse, spending your money unwisely. Yet to succeed and have self-confidence, you must make quality and BEST decisions.

TIP: When you are afraid of decisions you build up stress, create confusion, and make people wait. When you put off making decisions, you miss important opportunities.

If you are having trouble making decisions, talk to people you respect and who have the life you want. However, make the decision based on what *you* want, NOT what they tell you are the right things to do. Sometimes, too many opinions can create even more stress. Therefore, you should limit how many opinions you get about a given decision, and try to keep them to the people whose advice you trust for that topic. At the end of the day, listen to your gut on everything!

Decision-making is like playing cards. If you know the cards each player is holding, you make great decisions and win all the money. To make good decisions, you simply need enough information.

Life will throw so many challenges your way and you will not get it right all the time. However, this will build your decision-making muscle. You will start to see that you have created a positive pattern in making good choices.

15 QUESTIONS TO ANSWER BEFORE DECIDING

You can make all of your own decisions on your own. From <u>starting a business</u>, to <u>changing careers</u>, <u>buying a house</u> to <u>choosing a vacation</u>. Any decision is and can be really easy to make, following a couple of easy steps!

First, list all of your options. Once you have listed out your options, find the answers to these ***16 questions*** for each of your options. You will know some of these answers and can find out the others (as time goes on).

1. Somewhere along the line, your best correct decision will be obvious.

2. What is the goal or purpose of each option?

3. How do the purposes of each option align with your goals?

4. What are the statistics for each choice? Each of your options has statistics.

5. Finances? Two vital questions: What will each option cost? How much money will each return? *The cost is not a barrier if the predicted return is greater than the cost.*

6. Sequences? Most people forget to look at the exact steps involved with each solution. For example, you are notified by mail, "Congratulations! You have won either a deluxe AM/FM radio, $500 cash, a 60" TV or a cruise to Alaska!" You decide to go claim your prize. You never read the fine print or ask what steps are involved.

After a four-hour Mexico condo timeshare sales pitch, you get a coupon for a cheap radio.

7. Is this choice legal and ethical? Is it fair to everyone involved? Will you be proud of your choice in the future? Would you have any problem telling a judge or TV reporter about your choice?

8. What is the probability of success? Estimate the odds of success for each choice if you have no concrete data.

9. Do I have the resources? Resources include people, space, skill, knowledge, money and time. Do you have the necessary means for each choice?

10. What are the end results? If everything went smoothly, how would each choice turn out? What would the results be? How would it change things in a year or two? Also, consider the negative to see if you can live with them if that is the way that things are to turn out. Remember that even though you want things to turn out well, you need to consider both the good and the bad.

11. What do others want me to do and why? As your choice probably affects other people, you want to know what choice they want you to make. More importantly, *why* they want you to make it. Make a list of everyone who is affected and what you believe they want. You are not asking them to help with your decision, you are merely gathering information. If you are married, then your decision is now going to affect your family so that there are more people to consider when making your choice.

12. What are the potential gains and benefits? List each of these categories for each choice.

13. What are the potential losses and liabilities? Worst-case scenarios and risks? For each risk, look at how you can protect yourself or your group.

14. What are all the barriers and difficulties for each choice? What gets in the road of each choice? Lack of money? No one else wants it? Not enough time? Fear?

15. What would be easy and effortless about each choice? Some choices involve no barriers at all.

16. What do I really want? What am I willing to do? What interests me? Which choice turns me on and makes me happiest? Why do I feel like doing it?

This last question is the deal breaker. Interest and enthusiasm are vital to an option or personal choice ending up being *the 'right' decision.*

A mediocre (ok type) decision with lots of interest and enthusiasm, is more successful than a brilliant decision with no interest or enthusiasm.

You never regret a correct decision. It stands the test of time. A series of correct decisions will build your certainty and confidence. Once those around you learn you are mostly, if not usually right, they follow your lead without hesitation!

WHAT YOU SHOULD LEARN FROM THIS CHAPTER

Key-reminders and insights from Chapter 4, highlight:

• The decisions you make **today**, pave the way for the future you will be living **tomorrow**.

- There are **seven primary rules to good decision-making**. By following them carefully, you'll make a habit of them and good decision making will become a natural part of your everyday life.

- Good decision making relies on a **positive attitude**. If you are not making decisions with a positive outlook, then you will not be taking yourself down the right path with your choices.

- Working on your own self-confidence is an important part of the good decision making process. When you have strong self confidence, you are much better prepared to gauge the outcomes of different decisions, and to choose what is best for you.

- There are sixteen things that you should ask yourself before making any major decision. Answer them honestly, and look over the results to help guide you in the right direction.

Chapter 5

Forgiveness— The Key to a Happier and Longer Life

"To forgive is to set a prisoner free and discover that the prisoner was you."

–Lewis B. Smedes

I t is easy to say, "I forgive you" to someone who has wronged you. It is NOT however, easy to mean it! Oftentimes, we let this phrase slip out, to solve our problems in-the-moment and short-term, but, when we simply say it for the sake of ending an argument, the effects last: wounds remain, unhealed, and your quality of life and life-style suffers, to boot!

79

Forgiveness is an essential part of your life... *or it **should** be*. Your mind was not meant to harbor ill memories, nor your emotions to remain stagnated with anger. But, without forgiveness as an integral part of your life, that is what will happen if you refuse to let go of the wrongs done to you (not forget, but accept for your advantage), you will never be able to experience the joys of life. You will be too consumed with anger.

You must learn to forgive, to cultivate a lifestyle of goodwill. This is not to say that you should not experience darker emotions; they are part of you. But, to allow them to control you and your actions is definitely NOT the way. Instead, you must learn to control them. Only then will you reap the benefits of a 'forgiving' life:

- **Physiological**: Do not sneer. Holding onto negative thoughts and wishes does affect your body negatively. You can, literally, make yourself sick with these feelings. By focusing on wrongs done to you, you do not allow your mind the chance to absorb other stimulation, or even allow your body the chance to relax itself. You are bringing unneeded stress into your body. This will have an undeniable effect with long-term, future implications. With a forgiving attitude, however, you let your body and mind relax, and then move on. This is of the utmost importance.

- **Emotional:** The more obvious benefits of leading a 'forgiving life' is the emotional qualities and maturity that you will reach and showcase. If you continue to harbor grudges, or think only of retribution, you will ruin your emotional self (and, yes, there is such a thing!). Your quality of life will be tainted. Through forgiveness, however, you can learn to experience the world for every aspect of it, allowing yourself the emotional ability to appreciate it.

Forgiveness is a choice, and not an easy one. After all, if a wrong has been committed, why forgive it? Is that not simply condoning the action?

No!

You are not giving your permission to continue this wrong; you are not telling someone that they can keep doing it without fear of consequence. You are not forgetting what was done to you. You have simply learned to move away from it, to grow from it.

A GREAT EXAMPLE: OPRAH WINFREY

A very famous example of a forgiving woman who has used this positive lifestyle to live her life to its fullest, is Oprah Winfrey. Today, we know her as the multiple Emmy-Award-winning host of the Oprah Winfrey Show, as well as an Academy Award nominated actress, the influential book critic and magazine publisher. However, remember that she was not born into this lifestyle of success, attributed to the world's only female black billionaire. She created it herself, overcoming a number of hardships and setbacks along the way.

She has fought her way through rounds of criticisms and controversies, and has allowed herself to forgive, so that she can move on in a healthy, positive, and winning way.

Beyond the problems she had growing up, like living part of her childhood in a lower-class, rough neighborhood, and suffering because of a lack of a support structure, and even sexual abuse from her cousin, Oprah has also experienced challenging hurdles throughout her professional career.

In fact, when she changed the focus of her show mid-way through the 1990's, her successes caused many critics to blame her for popularizing "tabloid talk-shows". These critics pointed the finger at Oprah for making shows such as The Jenny Jones Show, Ricki Lake, and even The Jerry Springer Show as popular as they are. However, Oprah held her own, maintained her own focus, and accepted that people will criticize her when she is so visible to the public. She allowed herself to recognize that a person with as much success and fame as she will bound to be critiqued, and occasionally blamed for the actions of others—things that remain outside of her personal control.

Ben Shapiro took a stab at her when she showed her anti-war perspective on her show at the time leading up to the US-led invasion of Iraq. He wrote cutting remarks, and belittling statements about her opinions, her means of expression, and about her overall. He claimed that she is a *"dangerous political force... with unpredictable and mercurial attitudes toward the major issues of the day."* Still, Oprah continued with grace and forgiveness. Not once did this highly influential woman with her popular magazine and television show, bring herself down to the level of lashing out at Mr. Shapiro in the many ways that she could have done. Instead, she allowed her own integrity to speak for itself, and she continued to progress in the way that she felt was right for her.

As recently as 2006, rappers such as Ice Cube, 50 Cent, and Ludacris criticized Oprah for what they claimed to be an anti *hip-hop* attitude. Winfrey had indeed made a comment about hip-hop in an interview with GQ magazine, and she had quoted lyrics by Ludacris to substantiate her opinion.

Her claim, however, was NOT against the genre of hip-hop, but rather against lyrics that marginalize women. Instead of lashing out at these artists, she reiterated her point, and clarified that she does enjoy some hip-hop artists such as Kanye West. She then spoke in person with Ludacris to explain that she did understand that his music was for entertainment purposes, but that her concern was that some listeners may not understand that it is not to be taken literally.

I applaud Oprah for facing her critics with such style and grace. She has ample opportunity to seek vengeance on the people who choose to criticize her or cause her trouble, but she never stoops to that level. Instead, she either ignores the pests, allowing her integrity to speak for itself, or she explains her position in a clear and calm way that demonstrates her willingness to forgive, and move on in a healthy and appropriate way.

I find Oprah to be a tremendous example of how we can all live forgiving lifestyles in a way that helps us to be happy, healthy, and better as human beings.

KEEPING A POSITIVE FORGIVING ATTITUDE

"Blowing out another's candle will not make yours shine brighter."

—*Anonymous*

No one ever said, *"Life was easy"*, unless they were un-naturally lucky. Instead, most of us will admit that life has its good and bad moments, its highs and lows. Of course, staying positive for the highs is easy; everything goes your way—it is the low points that truly test your nature and character:

- *Do you have enough trust in yourself to remain positive in your life?*

- *Do you have enough faith in the power of forgiveness to see yourself through darker times?*

It is very easy to fall back on old grudges and re-open wounds. When times are tough, some rejoice in nursing their anger. This is not the way, however. Instead, you must learn to remain positive in your life—you must be able to cope through hard times, armed with the knowledge that it will not last.

To do that, you can follow some very simple steps. These can keep you on the right track...*away from anger:*

- **Take time for yourself.** The worst thing you can do during times of trouble is deny yourself time alone. Whether you spend it in prayer, meditation, or simply sitting on a park bench, let yourself digest the happenings of the day. You should never try to ignore them; this will only breed later heartache and anguish. Instead, go over your day and accept every aspect of it. Be positive, however, with your examinations. Use this time alone to calm yourself and remember that the day is almost over.

- **Watch what you say.** Whether you are entertaining guests at a Sunday barbecue, or out with family at the movies, you must be careful what you say. Your words carry weight, weight that can bring others down. Negative thoughts spread easily. Instead, try to boost the level of positive thinking in your group. Make love and optimism infectious.

- **Choose your friends wisely**. If you wish to maintain a positive outlook on life, you do not need to surround yourself with people who only see the bad. This will disrupt your attempts. Find people similar to yourself, those seeking an enriched lifestyle through forgiveness. This is not to say, of course, that you should shut out those who think differently, or keep them out of your life entirely. Not at all. That would go against the idea of forgiveness. Instead, try to enrich their days with YOUR positivity. You may just help them cope with whatever tragedies that they may be suffering from.

A Forgiving Lifestyle is Good for You!

Forgiveness should be looked upon as a gift you give to yourself. This makes forgiveness an inward act, as opposed to an outward act, merely for someone else's benefit. While the person you forgive may feel better, their feelings cannot match the joy you give yourself by your willingness to forgive.

Too often, we believe that, as the wounded party, we are entitled to hear the offender ask for forgiveness. Perhaps the true onus lies with the offended. If we have the grace to extend forgiveness where none is asked, we may find the burden of anger lifted from our hearts more readily.

That might, however, still be much easier said than done. Anger and resentment are easy to generate and maintain. Forgiveness requires effort and imagination. If you can imagine a future devoid of the anger, you can begin to feel forgiveness. A heart free of hurt and anger is more open to accepting and expressing positive emotions.

That is not to say you should never feel or express anger. If you feel wronged, you will benefit from expressing your feelings—if not to the offender, then to a third party willing to listen. Getting the feelings out is called venting, as in letting off the steam, releasing the pressure. If you cannot bring yourself to speak to someone, consider writing your feelings down, or speaking into a tape or voice-recorder (for your ears ONLY!).

Forget about the adage, "Forgive and forget." No one expects you to forget what happened. Nor should the offending party forget what they did. You both have to remember the circumstances of the problem, so you can avoid repeating the incident over and over again. *Remember what went wrong and remember how you got past the hurt.*

The important thing is to say what you are feeling, that the emotions do not get bottled up inside. Denying a problem does not contribute to a solution. Denial only leads to repressed emotions, which contribute to physical and psychological problems in the long-run. For one thing, you risk casting yourself in the role of the victim in perpetuity. You also taint your relationships, which cannot be healthy and productive, if you refuse to let go of negative emotions. If you want to increase your odds of living a long and healthy life, you have to address each and every issue that threatens your wellbeing.

Once you have given voice to your feelings, you are ready to tackle the more difficult task of forgiveness. It all comes down to making a conscious choice to forgive. Letting go of negative emotions is a healing process that releases internal pressures and literally lightens the mind.

Living a Lifestyle of Forgiving, Will Add Years to Your Life!

If you want to live a longer, healthier life, start by embracing the concept of forgiveness. You might be surprised by how much better you will feel.

People who hold grudges are more likely to develop headaches, ulcers, and other physical ailments, due to unreleased negative emotions that can actually produce toxins within the body. New research suggests that harboring feelings of betrayal may be linked to high blood pressure which can ultimately lead to stroke, kidney or heart failure, or even death.

There is a **simple three-step plan for achieving forgiveness**. It all starts with facing the problem head-on and allowing yourself to feel and express anger, rather than denying your emotions. Put yourself in the other person's shoes.

- *What motivated the offending behavior?*

- *Were there any extenuating circumstances?*

While you are not expected to make excuses for the other person, you cannot help but benefit from understanding another point of view.

The important thing is to say what you are feeling so the emotions do not get bottled up inside. Denying a problem does not contribute to a solution. Denial only leads to repressed emotions, which can make you sick!

Effects of Un-forgiveness on Health: Things Even Your Doctor May Not Know

Forgiving is an extremely important part of your everyday life. You have surely been told this since you were a very young child, but how many of us actually apply this to the way that we live as adults?

With today's fast-moving society that is always demanding more, and putting a great deal of strain and stress on our patience, it becomes quite a challenge to maintain that forgiving outlook on life. Well, in case you needed more motivation to try, researchers have now discovered that living a consistently forgiving lifestyle, is actually good for your physical health.

It has been discovered that people living a forgiving lifestyle also experience lower cases of heart disease, cancer, and autoimmune diseases (to name a few) due to the lower levels of stress experienced for this conscious choosing of forgiveness over bitterness and resentment, or harbored anger.

As you can see, it is extremely beneficial to your health to reduce the number of grudges that you hold, and begin making a regular habit of forgiving people whenever possible. This is not to say that you should become a doormat, because that is not what forgiving is all about. What it does mean, is that when someone says that they are sorry, and you believe that they mean it, forgive them, both by telling them that they are forgiven, and by meaning what you say!

You will feel much less stress, have a lighter overall view on life, and feel much more content about the world around you, and, as you can see, you have a healthier life while you're at it. Avoiding an unforgiving life, also therefore means avoiding much more than grudges—it is the emotional equivalent to an apple-a-day needed for regular health and happiness (to keep the doctor away!).

PLANNING FOR LIFE'S IRRITATIONS — LIFE HAPPENS

"Forgive your enemies, but never forget their names."

—John F. Kennedy

Everyone is searching for that cure-all, know-all plan. That one plan that will solve all difficulty and problems, making life easy... Unfortunately, such a plan does not exist. There is no perfect way to go through life. There is no one answer to all the questions. Life happens, and not always the way you want it to.

That does not, however, mean that you cannot plan for some of its more irritating moments. You can—just, perhaps, not the way you intended.

You will not always be in control. It's a simple phrase that few people remember. Sometimes, you just have to let things be. This does NOT mean to *roll over in defeat*; it just means to pick your battles more carefully. Some campaigns simply cannot be won, or should not be bothered with.

Learn to accept. Things are going to happen, things that you certainly never wanted. You can respond to these situations in two ways: (1) Get angry and refuse to let it go. (2) Acknowledge that some scenarios are unavoidable and do not lose your cool. Does the second option sound seemingly better? Well, it is! Most people forget it, however. It is much easier to get mad, but since when has easier, equaled right? You need to remember that you will not always be in control; accept that and things will move more smoothly.

Practice positive thinking. You cannot go through life staring through a cynic's eyes. *(Well, you could, but why would want to?)* Why ruin the quality of your day with dark thoughts? Instead, try to find lighter aspects. Positivity is not just saying, "It will be a good day." It is believing it and making it happen.

Forgiveness is essential. That sentence should be enough on its own that no explanation is needed. Sadly, many people do not grasp the concept of forgiving.

They would rather hold on to the memory of past wrongs and perceived injustices. This is a poor way to live! You ruin the quality of your life to the point that you have no life. You only have your dark ambitions. This is not the right way. Learn to forgive those who you feel wronged you; learn to accept the past as just that—the past. Focus on your future, not your need for revenge.

Life will not always be easy; it will not always be fair. But, if you can follow those simple steps, you can face it with a clearer mind and a lighter heart.

LEARNING TO FORGIVE AS A PART OF ANGER MANAGEMENT

"If ye forgive men their trespasses, your heavenly Father will also forgive you"

—Mt. 6:14

We all get angry; it is a truth never failing among the human race. We all know we should forgive, but it is another truth that many of us do not act upon or get to!

To forgive someone whom you believe has wronged you—or caused anger of any shade to appear—is to put it simply, NOT easy. No, the easy thing is to hold a grudge or seek retribution. The easy thing is to nurture those ill feelings.

But easy does not equal right.

You must learn to forgive those who caused you anger; to refuse to do so will only hurt you. Carrying pain in your mind clouds your judgment and emotions, refusing to let other sensations or experiences in. You block yourself from life.

So, what do you do? How do you curtail your anger and learn to forgive?

Understand what has made you angry. Every situation is different and you cannot simply loop it all together as "something bad". You need to be able to step away and examine. Knowing what caused the anger is the first step in stopping it.

Once you understand what has made you angry—whether it is the man who stole the parking spot you had been waiting on for five minutes, or the woman you caught gossiping about you in the office cafeteria—you can know how to deal with it. It is not an easy thing to examine your emotions, especially ones this strong, but it is necessary.

Decide how best to react to a situation. Anger is going to happen. There is no denying that. But, how you chose to *express it* makes all the difference. Throwing things or trying to pick a fight with the cause of your pain, is not the wisest of moves. Instead, find another outlet that allows you to channel your anger elsewhere *(whether you go for a run, begin a new project, etc)*. Vent your frustrations through other means.

Once you have let go of your anger, you can approach the cause with a steadier outlook. The worst thing you can do is try to debate the questions of right and wrong while angry. Instead, you talk with composure. Of course, you may not wish to speak with this person—or even have the chance—but, if you do wish to speak with them, it must be done calmly. Explain your position: Why were you angry? Why were you hurt? Note the "were" (past tense), in that previous sentence. You may still be hurt from whatever happened, but the anger should be dissipating.

Forgive. Whether the persons who have wronged you are seeking forgiveness or not, you need to do it. This is not simply them offering an apology and you accepting; this is letting go of the past. Forgiveness will bring you peace. Holding grudges and refusing to let a memory die, will only hurt you. It will make you angry at everything because you will be constantly reminded of it. Instead, learn to shrug off causes of anger. Accept them, express them, and then move on.

FORGIVING HEALS FAMILIES' WOUNDS

"We read that we ought to forgive our enemies; but we do not read that we ought to forgive our friends."

—Sir Francis Bacon

The need for forgiveness impacts all relationships in our lives. This is not simply a balm for romantic woes. We also experience conflict with parents, siblings, friends and associates. Those relationships require the same care and attention as any romantic entanglements in which we may find ourselves.

We cannot choose our families, but we can choose how we handle family dynamics. Healthy family relationships rely on the power of forgiveness.

In many families, conflicts arise between parent and child (at any age). Lingering resentments grow out of childhood hurts and affect adult behavior. By exploring our relationships with our parents, we can learn to understand and strive for forgiveness.

Childhood issues may be as "simple" as a one-time critical remark from a parent, or as complex as child abuse over the course of several years. In any case, the ramifications last long past and beyond childhood.

Adults who experience difficulty maintaining healthy relationships, or who are not achieving career success, often find their problems correlate with personal issues rooted in childhood.

As in any relationship, forgiveness in families is key to maintaining healthy interactions. Even so-called dysfunctional families can overcome their problems by learning to let go of the hurt.

Denying a problem does not contribute to a solution. Denial only leads to repressed emotions and ill health. If you want to re-establish a healthy family dynamic, you have to address each and every issue that threatens its stability.

The offended party, having been made to feel victimized, wants nothing more than to turn the tables and take control. Withholding forgiveness, is a way of wielding power over the offender. However, that power position is damaging to both parties, over the longer term. The offender, in essence, lives in a perpetual state of penitence, while the offended holds on to physically and psychologically damaging anger.

Once you have given voice to your feelings, you are ready to tackle the more difficult task of forgiveness. It all comes down to making a conscious choice to forgive. Letting go of negative emotions is a healing process that releases internal pressures and literally lightens the mind.

FORGIVING WILL ENHANCE YOUR RELATIONSHIPS

"To forgive is the highest, most beautiful form of love. In return, you will receive untold peace and happiness."

—Robert Muller

Forgiveness and unconditional love walk hand-in-hand through our relationships. Mother Theresa summed up that belief when she said, ***"If we really want to love, we must learn how to forgive."***

The need for forgiveness impacts all relationships in our lives. This is not simply a balm for romantic woes. We also experience conflict with parents, siblings, friends and associates. Those relationships require the same care and attention, as any romantic entanglements in which we may find ourselves.

Having relationships opens us up to getting hurt. The more people we know and care for, the greater the chance one of them will do something to offend us at some point. This is not indicative of poor taste in friends or bad luck in the family to which you born. Rather, this simply indicates a fundamental truth of human nature. We are flawed beings, fully capable of causing hurt, whether intentional or not, to those we love.

We are also individuals. No two people are exactly alike in mannerisms or desires. We each have our own priorities and preferences. Conflicts may arise when the priorities of one or more people do not coincide. We cannot always resolve our problems through compromise. Even when we do, some or all parties will probably give up something, or be left doing things they would rather not do!

Friends, for instance, might argue about how to spend a Saturday night, while co-workers may come to an impasse over office procedures. Deal with the conflict directly; state your point of view firmly yet fairly. Next, find a way to move on. After all, you still have to be able to interact with these people long after the conflict has any real meaning. True friends are not going anywhere, and co-workers remain—unless someone gets a new job—so do not hang onto the conflict indefinitely.

If a relationship is truly important to you, it is it NOT worth every effort to make it work? You can overcome conflicts with those closest to you, if you just allow for the possibility of forgiveness.

Forgiveness In The Work Place

You hear laughter and hushed voices; you poke your head out of your cubicle to see what holds so many of your coworkers' attention, always happy to hear a good joke… Your eyes widen as you see them, gathered by the water cooler, mocking some of your famous hand gestures. One is even throwing on an accent very similar to yours.

What do you do?

Your first thought could be to get out of your cubicle, walk with great purpose to the water cooler, get yourself a drink and then throw it in their faces. You can picture yourself standing triumphant as they drip away, embarrassed to have ever mocked you.

Your second thought could be to simply stick your head back in your cubicle and pretend you did not hear them, only to shoot an angry stare as they walk by. Or, perhaps say something cryptic to let them know that you know.

If either one of these ideas sounded like a good one, keep reading.

The workplace is filled with gossip and distrust. It is human nature at its most competitive. Tempers will flare and egos will bruise. What you must learn is how to deal with these types of challenges, realities and problems through forgiveness.

This is not to say that you are to take everything people throw at you with a smile, refusing to defend yourself. No, that is not forgiveness. What forgiveness entails is learning to accept problems as inevitable and making sure they don't bring you down. When you choose to forgive a coworker (or coworkers) that have wronged you, you let yourself move past the problem. You are no longer burdened with anger, or wasting your time seeking revenge; instead, you can devote your energies to projects and things that need to be finished and get done.

Forgiveness is when you can move away from a problem. Get angry, express that anger through positive ways, and then focus on something else. You no longer have to harbor darker thoughts. You can see the situation clearly. And this is a necessary thing in the workplace.

When you deal with people, there will be problems. This is a truth you must learn to accept. That is why forgiveness is so essential. Why waste your career worried about what others have said? Yes, it hurts. Yes, you deserve to be angry. But, after the initial feeling, you must learn to forgive their stupidity and move on. Otherwise, you will only hurt yourself.

WHAT YOU SHOULD LEARN FROM THIS CHAPTER

Key-reminders and insights from Chapter 5, highlight:

- Forgiveness is not an easy thing to do, but it is a very important part of your life.

- Forgiving is a vital part of achieving your best possible emotional and physiological health.

- There are many things that you can do to help to achieve a positive outlook that makes forgiving a natural part of your life.

- By living a forgiving lifestyle, you may add years to your life. Conversely, by resisting being a forgiving person, you put yourself at risk for a number of health issues such as heart problems, cancers, and other stress-related problems.

- One of the first steps to living a forgiving lifestyle is, to realize that life will happen, and it is not always great. Therefore, it is best to prepare yourself with actions and attitudes that will help you to accept that your life—and the people in it—will not always be perfect, but it does NOT mean that they are not worthy of forgiveness.

- Forgiving will have an extremely positive impact on your relationships, family, and working life.

Personal Exercise

Write down the names of the people who have hurt you and who you feel that you need to forgive. Below each name, leave some space for you to think about— and write down... *the ways in which your life would be different if you decide right this second to forgive that person and move on with your life.*

Chapter 6

The Sisterhood
Now, Now Ladies. Can We NOT <u>ALL</u> Just Get Along?

"For there is no friend like a sister, in calm or stormy weather, to cheer one on the tedious way, to fetch one if one goes astray, to lift one if one totters down, to strengthen whilst one stands."

—Christina Rossetti

Mean girls. Catfights. Queen bees…?!
There are many different ways to describe the way that women can be jealous, envious and all-around nasty to and with one another. By the time a young girl is eleven years old, she might very well already 'know' what *type* or category she falls into or would be stereotyped as.

Is she the brainy one? The athlete? Or the popular one? These labels can very well direly affect both psyche and self-esteem, which girls can often carry throughout their lives—including when they enter the workplace or find their first employment, or take a professional step towards realizing their dreams.

Girls learn early-on that there are just so many good-looking boys to go around and that not everyone can be popular or beautiful. This is society's messaging, however right or wrong this might seem.

When resources are limited, we compete! That is the long-and-short of it. We fight very hard to get what we want. It creates competition around every corner, along with envy and jealousy.

If someone is at the top of the heap or ladder, it is so very hard to stay there. The pressure only keeps retching up in high school. Whosoever is at the top, is always ready and watching for someone to knock them off their roost, so to speak. This is the ugly reality of the competitive culture of entitlement we are raised in and growing up to compete in. There is no denying it. Ask anyone that has or is living it… we all know the truth here.

FACT: It is exactly this kind of thinking that can also easily turn us against one another. Leaving us to grow up thinking that women are the enemies in our lives, when really it is our very own insecurities that might be playing tricks on us. The very things that allow us to miss some of the greatest and most rewarding relationships possible potentially.

As women, I think that we need to learn to support one another's dreams and ambitions. That is NOT to say that you should trust every woman that you meet, because you simply cannot and should not!

However, now that you are taking all of the steps in this book to better yourself, you will begin to read people and their very character early on. Armed with this knowledge, you can therefore more easily decide for yourself, if someone that you get to know, has the right motivations and intentions, as far as and where you are concerned.

After all, as women, we share many of the same struggles and concerns and it would serve us better to help one another, rather then acting like prima-donnas, or drama-queens, gossiping and saying negative things that ultimately cut-down and hurt others (even ourselves in the process).

Remember, what goes around comes around! Just as you want to have great women in your life that believe in you and want the best for you, you must start with yourself now, for once! Decide that you are going to start treating other women properly, with the respect they deserve. If you start doing this, you will begin to notice that positive people will migrate into your life and you will feel enriched and more confident, in, around and with your friends.

FACT: THIS CHANGE HAS TO START WITH YOU! You see, one of the main differences between men and women, is the way we think. Typically, women will choose friends with whom they feel an emotional bond, while men will select companions who share similar interests. In general, the emotional connection—while there in both cases—is expressed and pursued VERY DIFFERENTLY, in the friendships of men and of women. These discerningly different drivers can easily be overlooked, misinterpreted or dismissed—wrongfully so!

Though it would be easy to assume that women would be the most competitive in male-dominated industries, it has, in fact, been discovered that women compete the most in traditional women's subjects, and are less "catty", when it comes to traditional male roles.

On the other hand, when stepping into a role traditionally held by men—for example, a substantial corporate position, say—women, will frequently take on a somewhat "male" posturing or competitive attitude, in order to keep up with their male counterparts and surpass any stereotypes or assumptions that may be held about their abilities to perform in a position and ability to "climb the proverbial ladder".

The same can be said about *tokenism*. Women all know about these spots that have been set aside, and will take on a "male competitive" nature, in order to translate into realizing the select few who will obtain these coveted positions.

Women have so many more opportunities today than they have had in the *not-so-distant* past. Women, who realize that men will not—and, for that matter, should not feel obligated to help them get ahead, will soon realize it and will be better able to help each other. It is in their own mutual best interest!

They are so much more independent. They can exude and have a confidence level that simply was not there before, in the workplace, at home, all-round—much has changed!

It is not just an "age" thing, though. While women do have a tendency to unite, they are also the most skilled at being mean and cutting.

SIDEBAR: I remember the meanest kids that I dealt with in grade school, middle school, and high school, were all girls. That is NOT surprising at all. Have a look at the new reality shows on MTV that highlight actual high schools. All you see is constant drama, hurt feelings, backstabbing, and stealing boyfriends. Yet, have you ever noticed that, for the most part, the guys pretty much get along—or at least tolerate—one another?

So the real question remains: *Why is it that the girls talk constantly, trying to put and pull one another down?*

The answer: survival! We are all fighting for our share of attention; and in high school, let us just face it… it is all about the boys and wanting to be the best.

Unfortunately, when it comes down to it, we DO NOT particularly care whose lives we have to ruin to get there, in the process!

However, this is also NOT the BEST way to achieve what we want, since everything else in life does not work the same way as in high school. In the "Real World", if you continue this behavior long enough, it becomes a really bad habit, second nature if you will. You will find people do not want to be around you if you keep acting this way. Why? Well, it is simple! You have now officially become 'the' __*itch*! (pick your poison!)

It is similar to some statements made earlier, when we alluded to 'karma'. Everything that you have done in life will come around again to you, to ensure balance and fairness.

I will never forget what happened to me in the ninth grade. I came to school early one morning to meet up with my older friends. They were juniors and seniors and we hung out in a group of five. All of my friends were pretty and popular, *but I was the youngest.*

I became really good friends with this guy "RB" at school, and one of my good girl friends had a secret crush on him. Well, I did not know about it and he and I hung out all the time. She was so angry at me that she decided to yell at me in front of the entire first-period lunch-group. She argued that I should not think so much of myself, and that I had actually known how much she liked him, and that I was only trying to keep her from him. She simply carried on and on....

Needless so say, I was completely embarrassed and felt deeply betrayed and utterly humiliated. Even worse, I had had no idea that she was interested in him! I remember that I wanted to leave school and never come back.

Consequently, like all things in high school, this too passed and we were friends again the following week. My point is, that we are so quick to hurt one another and judge indiscriminately. Usually at the end of the day, it is your girl-friends that will be with you in YOUR most important times of need.

I know that in my life, I have met women with whom I have wanted to have a friendship, but where they have had no interest in giving me a chance at all. It was NOT reciprocal, mutually desired! For whatever reason, they were simply NOT willing to get to know me. You can probably relate to this situation, and the real truth is that this is the case most of the time, not so uncommon! The rule, rather than the exception.

Unfortunately too, this is generally rooted in their own jealousy and insecurities that they have yet to manage for themselves. Therefore, the fact is, it had nothing to do with *me—or you—personally*, but it had EVERYTHING to do with THEM! *(they/we just did not realize or see it yet for what it is!)*

Now, there are ways to handle this type of behavior.

First of all, recognize that **it is NOT you** (unless you are actually behaving inappropriately). But if you are trying to be kind and you just can not get through to them, take a step back, bless them, and move on.

Realize that you **CANNOT earn friendship with everyone and not everyone will see the good things about you**. *(Sometimes, people will look for the bad or create a false image in their mind that they buy into just to make themselves feel better about who they are—and who they wish they were).*

Again, this has nothing to do with you and everything to do with them. If you find that this person is in your family or is a family friend, then you may find it very difficult to be around them. If this is the case, do your best to limit your association with them and when you are around them, simply be nice and try not to focus on them. Instead, enjoy the other people with whom you do get along.

Sometimes, people will see that over the years they were wrong about you. Maybe at that time, a friendship may occur. But if not, there is no reason to speak badly about them. Take the high road. Remember that you are a person with character and dignity, and you do NOT need to lower yourself to their standards of being or living!

Think about **how you treat your girl-friends**. *Are you loyal, or do you back stab? Do you help your friends, or do you engage in a little gossip at their expense because it makes you feel better about yourself?*

When others talk about them do you join in or do you defend them? These are all really important character issues and this type of behavior—good, bad (and ugly)—will follow you into the workplace!

Women have more opportunities open to them now than ever before. That much is true. It is, however, also extremely important to be able to conquer the workplace and also make long-lasting friends, so that you remain fellows, friendly and part of the 'sister-hood' with women, and not rivals, against women!

Yes, I think that healthy competition is great, if it is done properly. It can help motivate both you and your friends to mature and develop, taking things to the next level. You will be able to inspire one another to reach a little higher for the next goal.

TIP: You should NEVER use your power to hurt or hinder another person's growth. This is NOT what will bring health, happiness and prosperity into your life. This is what will keep you from growing into the most empowered person that you can become! Ultimately you should always enrich, enable, enhance and advance one another!

A successful life is one of purpose and happiness. Yes, we all want to have beautiful things, look great, get attention; that goes without saying. However, I also know and realize, that you can have everything you want in life, while still having women-friends that stand by you and admire you… those that count you among their blessings. Now does not that sound MORE like the kind of life (and friends) that you do want?

The following is a *case-in-point* illustration of someone who has handled relationships with women very well. She has managed to bring her life and dreams into fruition, beyond the nature (and oftentimes challenging limitations or shortcomings) of the fashion industry. Here, where women are competing at the highest levels, clearly, she has done something right in the area of relationships. Let us take a closer look at this strong businesswoman.

A GREAT EXAMPLE: KIMORA LEE SIMMONS

Kimora Lee Simmons (nee Kimora Perkins), a former fashion model (who started young at 13 as a model for Coco Chanel), is now the head of design for the highly successful *Baby Phat*.

She is a tremendous example of somebody who took, addressed and overcame the obstacles in her life, in order to achieve what she wanted from it and then some. She is highly successful, ambitious and diligent.

After all, though she had little experience in the fashion industry aside from her modeling career, and had no fashion design background, she was able to take her former career, and her marriage to Russell Simmons (of Def Jam fame) and create a fashion business of incredible popularity, scope and depth, to great success.

Kimora's life has been challenging since birth. She grew up in a home where her father was a convicted felon and who served time in a Federal Prison for drug offenses and charges. This led to continual financial issues in her home, despite the fact that her mother had a well-paying job with the Social Security Administration. Little did she know that her two racial backgrounds and extreme height—5"10 at ten years old, and 6' by fourteen years old—would help her to begin a profitable professional modeling career!

This career started at thirteen years old, to assist her mother's financial troubles. When she had reached her full mature height at fourteen years old, she became a muse for Karl Lagerfeld (of the House of Chanel).

Though she achieved only her high school education—her academic career being cut into by her modeling career—she is very much an advocate of continuing education, and has donated large amounts of money to causes focused on overcoming educational deficiencies.

It was her marriage to Russel Simmons, and their two children, that would become the inspiration for the *Kimora Baby Phat Kids Collection.* Kimora was not, however, the founder of **Baby Phat**, as many would believe. This company, called Phat Farm, was actually already in existence, having been founded by Russel Simmons. It was the **Baby Phat** design that was created by Kimora, and she became creative director for that clothing-line, label and brand.

Kimora's real achievement is her ability to see potential in a situation. She takes acceptable risks and is able to draw success from situations that would cause others to flounder. It is NOT hard to use Kimora as an example of what a truly successful woman is all about. Her tenacity, creativity and perseverance continue to inspire many, from inside and outside the world of fashion and design.

Throughout her career, she had to deal with jealously and envy, but she also was able to maintain real relationships and friendships, despite these complexities and challenges.

Just because you are able to get to the top of the ladder in life/career, DOES NOT mean that you have to hurt or destroy others around you just to get there, or while you are on your way up!

Kimora leads by example, showcasing her strong work-ethic and loyalty, work-life balance, raising her new son, Kenzo Lee Hounsou, born May 30, 2009, (the first with actor and model Djimon Hounsou), celebrating and enjoying her new life. She filed for divorce in March 2008, (finalized in January, 2009), which had its own set of challenges.

A television-celebrity / judge on America's Next Top Model, she also has her renowned Reality TV Show called "Kimora: Life in the Fab Lane" on The E! Channel and Style Network (2007), while raising three children. She reaches out doing charitable work, fundraisers, through bodies like the Kimora Lee Simmons Scholarship Fund for college tuition support for academically successful girls with financial needs.

She is also a very supportive advocate, voice and spokesperson for grass-roots interest groups like Amfar, The G&P Foundation, Keep a Child Alive, Hetrick-Martin Institute and Rush Philanthropic.

Truly, in a sense, she is that modern epitome of the successful, multi-faceted, self-made woman! However, she also does not forget how or who to draw close and near when they are needed to bring and show support! A mogul, model, a mother, a friend to many, her star shines bright!

Let us indulge in a little love amongst one another. Take an opportunity to tell your girlfriends what they really mean to you.

- Have a special night out when all the girls get together and build one another up.

- If you realize that you do not have anyone in your life to call, chances are you need to look inside at your behavior to see what is keeping you from being a friend to someone and having beautiful relationships with other women. *(Do not be fooled into thinking that you can get through this life without some good girl friends)*

    You will be the one missing out, BIG TIME!

- If you find yourself surrounded by the wrong group of friends or no friends at all, you need to take accountability and decide today that you are going to make a positive shift in your life to start attracting the right group of people into your world.

SELF ESTEEM AND SELF CONFIDENCE: HOW TO GET IT

Self-esteem is about the most important thing that every girl *(and women in general—of all ages!)* needs to have. Yet, it seems that many of us out there not only DO NOT have it, but have NO idea HOW to get it!

Here is the good news: self-esteem and self-confidence CAN be learned and gained… ALL you have to do is simply apply the techniques into your daily life and you will begin to grow it. (Stay tuned to learn more on the HOW TO's)!

SIDEBAR: Just like watering your favorite plant, you need to nurture the right positive thinking into your daily life. Work to feed your self-esteem and boost your confidence. Without doing this, your confidence will either die or cease to exist at all, leaving you with low self esteem. Terrible things can creep into our lives when we do not honor ourselves (enough or at all!), NOT putting the right amount of self worth into our lives. This can only lead to DISASTER!

The first thing that you have to do is come to expect and accept that you are a **spiritual being that dwells within a human body** and although we can change many things that we do not like about ourselves physically, whether through diet, and/or working out—and then, of course, through a more extreme approach of elective cosmetic surgery (heaven forbid for the wrong reasons!)—we all, each and every one of us, has to understand that there are some things that you just cannot change! For example: *the shape of your body.*

If you have short legs you really cannot stretch them out to be the length of a super-model. This is something that is beyond your control, so you should decide that from this moment on, you are simply going to love the legs that you do have. Now, you can always improve upon how toned and lean they are, BUT you CANNOT change your bone structure! That is the gift that God, nature and genetics, intended and gave you!

I am talking about the physical features and challenges first-and-foremost, because we are taught early on that that part of our worth seems to be measured by ***the way we look***! For example, *when making a first impression.* Our 'worth' is NOT measured by outward appearance at all! I have known many women who were drop-dead gorgeous and were also among the most self-destructive; NOT only in the way they treat others, but by the way they secretly treated themselves.

It is a crying shame. The old saying "beauty comes from within" is just as true now as it was when it was first spoken. You can be beautiful on the outside and behave in an ugly way, or you can be a beautiful person overall, by behaving in a lovely way. ***You can learn to love the way you look, as well the way you feel about who you are, because this is what will create healthy self-esteem and confidence.***

Today, as women, we are bombarded by the media and made to feel as though we are all being judged in the World's Beauty Pageants! We are constantly being compared to one another and feeling as if we are not quite making the cut. This is one of the main reasons that women today have a lack of self-esteem. They simply DO NOT feel like they are ever pretty enough, or young enough or even attractive enough.

So what is a girl to do? We all know that the media will NEVER stop showing us the new hot line-up, coming faces and bodies of the year. First of all, you have to get your mind around the idea that the entire purpose of the beauty industry, is to generate sales for companies and make money. The more they flaunt the new flavor-of-the-month girl, the more money you will spend to look like her—*or at least try to. THEY ARE COUNTING, BETTING AND BARGAINING ON IT!*

So we in turn, as women (and some men), become obsessed with spending money that we do not have, and many of us fall into unhealthy eating habits and/or disorders, because we do not have the simple discipline or the know-how, practical knowledge, to do things the right way!

We continue or start to put our lives at risk and in the end we are still not happy with ourselves—NEITHER on the inside, OR the outside. You will never get the perfect look or feel the best about yourself when you engage in unhealthy behaviors, habits or patterns, for the wrong reasons!

This is such an important thing to talk about, because if you understand that some of the choices that you are making stem from a lack of self-esteem and low to no self-confidence, then you can be aware that you need to make a mental shift and begin to do things differently, today!

DO NOT get upset because you have just discovered that I am talking about you! Realize that you are now aware that there is a danger in feeling worthless, or feeling that you do not truly deserve good things. Notice these things now, so you can start to fix them… **Believe me they can be fixed!** THERE IS ALWAYS HOPE AND HELP (closer than you may think!).

I know that for me, being in the modeling industry, we are held to the highest level of judgment and competition—CONSTANTLY! Being rejected is something that models have to go through all the time (and yes, it does not get any easier, gals!).

> **SIDEBAR:** I simply had to decide early on—and get it clear in my mind –that if I did not get a modeling job, it was not because I was not pretty enough, or thin enough, it was that the client had a different idea of what they were looking for. That is the ONLY way to handle the world of modeling. You cannot take it personally! IT IS NOT PERSONAL!

I, like so many of you, have had to deal with issues that began as a young girl. It could be one statement made by a family member, or something you heard someone say about you when they didn't know you were listening.

I had so many issues because of my parents divorce. I certainly felt like I was to blame (even though I was not). I began to feel insecure about the way that I looked when my dad would talk about beautiful women. I always wondered if I was going to be beautiful. I just knew that there was a real importance placed on the way you look. But I also knew that I was interested in other things; not just the way I looked. I wanted to be smart and create a great life for myself.

Looking good will only get you so far in life and then you have to show others that there is something more to you than merely meets the eye at first glance. If you do not grow in other areas—if you only focus on shallow things—then that is all you will have in return.

With this in mind, I started reading self-help books (like this one) at a very young age. I actively sought out any useful information that was out there, to help better understand some of the things that I was thinking or going through.

I did not always tell my family the things that I dealt with because I am, by nature, a very private person. I kept most of it to myself. I thought that I could help myself. But NOT everyone can do it for themselves. In almost every case, it is better, and more effective to work through thoughts, issues, and problems **with someone else**, rather than trying to conquer everything alone. *(I read all that I could about self-esteem and how to get it. I realized that I could have it and I learned the techniques to get it, (just as you are learning now)!*

How I learned to develop my own self-esteem was to **start to value the gifts and talents that God gave me**. I decided to be thankful for what I had and not concentrate on the things I did not have.

You have to **find something that you enjoy doing,** even if it is not your life-long dream or life-goal. Working every day and accomplishing something, will help you start to feel good about yourself. That is when you decide what it is you really want to do in life. You can begin to dream and set achievable goals. Then, every time you reach a new goal, you will see that your confidence builds and your self-esteem will grow.

Try new things often and see what you like. Parents, when they have young kids, do this all the time. They register little Peter in three different sports teams, so they can see what he is good at and which one he is drawn to. This is just what we need to do for ourselves as adults. Who knows what you will learn about yourself? DARE TO TAKE A CHANCE!

You have to **be open to new things and suggestions from others**. Take chances, for at the end of the day you may gain a new hobby or find a new passion. YOU NEVER KNOW! Look at each new experience—whether you have liked it or not—as just one more step to building a more confident you!

Not everything that you do will have purpose and meaning, but **if you stop trying, then you will not grow**. If there is something you have always wanted to do, *make it happen*. Find a way to accomplish that goal. Set a time frame around it and go for it. Who knows? Maybe you will be great at it and love it! **Whatever it is that makes you smile and is good for you, get more of it. Go after life or it will pass you by.**

You see, we all start out not feeling as though we are good enough, but each one of us has to decide that we are going to take control over those negative thoughts and start changing our lives for the better. **It is a conscious decision and one that only you can make.**

The people around you can influence you, but ultimately, it is your decision! Whether you will or will not take control and do what is best for you, is entirely up to you. There is something very reassuring and affirming about this!

Every time you wake up and declare that this is going to be a great day and something wonderful is going to happen to you today, every time that you follow that up with writing out your goals and your affirmation, saying them out loud— **you begin to feel empowered and you will begin to believe that good things really are going to happen for you.**

You will also begin to realize that you deserve good things once you believe this about yourself. There is no stopping you! Watch out world, here you come!!! Hear me roar!!!!!!!!

Once you start to activate those powerful universal laws, you will **begin to change and grow.** Again, think of your self-esteem and self-confidence, as you would a new plant that needs to be taken care of in order to grow.

You have to become a **disciplined thinker** and **not allow yourself to fall into the trap of negativity.** You will have days when you feel bad, upset, or angry—we all do and that is life—IT IS NORMAL! However, try to have more days in which you feel happy, and that will keep you on the right course.

Here are some examples of things people do that have low self-esteem. I want to highlight them, in order for you to see IF they apply to you. **(Once you realize this about yourself you can start to make the changes.)**

- **Negative self-talk**—"I could never be good enough to do that".

- **Blaming bad luck**—"She always gets the best luck, and I am always stuck with this mess".

- **Blaming the past**—"I would be doing really well if I had never met So-and-So who messed everything up for me".

- **Wishing with no action**—"I wish I could have a great job. Oh well... I am off to the job that I hate".

- **Waiting for the impossible to make a change**—"I will be able to straighten everything out… as soon as I win the lottery".

Now, here are examples of things that YOU can do NOW, to start building your *self-esteem:*

Write out **_ten things_** that you like about yourself *(it can be anything from your eyes to your sense of humor. Be creative when you are making the list and really give it some thought).*

Now that you have your list, take a mirror and begin to tell yourself the following things aloud:

- I am beautiful

- I am ambitious,

- Start telling yourself all the things that made your list—do this every day for a month (** NOTE: At the end of the month, you will begin to see a change in how you feel about yourself).

- This is NOT arrogant at all. You are starting to develop and realize your self worth. Do not SELF-SABOTAGE or let anyone take that from you; especially yourself!

- Start complimenting others on the things that you see in them that are GREAT—even if you DO NOT know them.

- Smile when you pass by others. *(You never know what that smile can do for someone who is feeling down).*

- If you see someone that has beautiful eyes, tell them, let them know! It will make them feel great, but you get the real blessing.

- Practice more patience! We all hate to wait in lines, but sometimes that is the way it goes. We do not all get the red-carpet treatment and that is okay too.

- Take a deep breath and crack a joke, lighten the mood around you.

- Good deeds DO NOT go unnoticed. Do what you can if you see an opportunity to help someone.

- If you are at the gas pump and an elderly woman drives up looking as though she does not have the strength to pump her gas, offer to do it for her. Be her angel for the moment.

All these seemingly 'little' things, oftentimes overlooked, will bless you in ways that you do not even know. 'Karma' is watching and when you need a break, something good in return occurs MOST of the time! It will come to you, especially if you have gone out of your way to help others *(at least, that is how the philosophy goes and advocates!)*.

If you begin to do these simple things today, I promise you, you will have a life of self-worth and immense inner-value. Do not settle for average or mediocre!

Be bold! Be great! Find your passion and create your destiny! God gave you the desires of your heart so you could achieve them, not to let them lay dormant in your mind. Being great takes hard work, but it is also SO well worth the effort!

Please take a chance on YOU for once. I believe that YOU CAN do it!

THE IMPORTANCE OF FRIENDSHIP AMONG WOMEN

"There is a special kind of freedom sisters enjoy. Freedom to share innermost thoughts, to ask a favor, to show their feelings. The freedom is simply to be themselves."

—Unknown

What would we do without our girlfriends? Guys have their poker-pals and golf or fishing, working, hunting and drinking buddies. Plenty of married couples call their spouse their best friend. But close friendships among women are, well, just that… a whole heck of a lot different and totally worthwhile!

AN INTERESTING FACT: Sixty four percent of women choose to talk to girlfriends rather than their spouses or mothers about relationships and sex. These revelations come as no surprise to researchers who have studied women's' friendships.

SIDEBAR: My best friends are so important to me that I can barely quantify our relationships and do them justice in the process. I can be so honest here, with and about them, without any fear or risk of the relationships being damaged or hurt in any way. Between us, there is no fear at all. We just understand what the other person is going through. After all, many of us share the same issues.

I have chosen friends who have each of our best interests at heart, front of mind and are happy when something great happens in each other's lives. We cheer one another on and lend a hand, whenever and wherever help is needed. That is what a good girl friend does, after-all.

That *depth of emotion* and *lack of fear*, are the essence of what makes women's' friendships ***different than men's***. In general, men's friendships are based on common interests or skills (as I mentioned before)—a shared commonality of sorts. On the other hand, women's' friendships, relationships and connections are based on sharing feelings and emotions. All of this does not necessarily mean that men's' friendships with other men are any less in-depth, treasured or relevant. They are just VERY DIFFERENT. Regardless, friendships may very well be just as important and enduring, but the degree of emotional reliance and caring tends to be more implicit than explicit in the case of the women.

Women are far more likely than men to join formal or informal support groups, in order to help one another deal with issues, for anything ranging from and including child care and/or work, social, emotional even relationship problems.

However, women's' friendships can be more volatile than men's', as well. This happens because, at times, they are more intense in a manner of speaking.

In general, females may expect more time and emotional attention from their girlfriends than men do from their male friends. Women also are more likely to "carry issues" and hold grudges. It can get complex fast!

These connections and differences are also increasingly becoming even more important in a society in which a growing number of people are single, (either by choice or circumstances).

By 2010, it is projected that 31 million Americans will live alone.

All of these factors make friendship MORE critical than ever. Every woman that I know, that is currently single, is out there looking for "Mr. Right". Sure, they may say that they are happy being alone and that the time is good for them, yet they are all on dating websites and/or searching to be set up on dates.

I completely understand that they want to find the right guy, for we are certainly NOT made for or meant to be alone. God created Adam and Eve and if we were meant to be alone, then Adam would have been so, and content! Yet, all the animals were also put in pairs, both male and female. It goes without saying then, that we are meant to be together, almost BY OUR VERY DESIGN!

This is also were it can get quite 'sticky' and complex. It seems like there are more women out there looking for love, than there are great men to go around!

This is where competition and jealousy start. I believe that every one of us has that "special someone" out there. I know it sounds incredibly cliché, but I think and believe it to be very true, indeed! The time in my life that I was NOT looking for Mr. Right was the time that "Mr. Right" came into my life! *(you just never know when it is going to happen for YOU!)*

Ladies, instead of concentrating on tearing one another down, or apart, rather put that energy into being the best that you can be. Get in shape, change that negative attitude into one that a guy will want to be around! If he should feel great when he is with you and if he feels great around you, he will never want to be without you! It is that simple, really. However, very few women figure this one out early on, or when it matters most. STOP MISSING OUT!

Guys are definitely drawn to women by the physical and outer beauty initially. However, a man will stay with you forever, IF you make him feel good about himself. This is a mysterious fact many women do not quite understand. *(We will talk more about the issue of MEN specifically, later in the book, so stay tuned.!)*

The Other Woman in Your Life: Your Mother

Call her what you will—mom, mother, *mommy dearest*—we all have a mother. She can be different things to different people. She can range from being the greatest joy and blessing in our lives perhaps, to the greatest challenge we may face, in life. *(Remember of course, this is most likely also how our mothers see us, too!)* I want to talk a little bit about the incredible relationship you have with your mom.

If you are anything or even a little like me, then you have a very close relationship with your mother and you completely enjoy one another. Now that I am an adult, my relationship with my mom is better than ever.

Of course, being a teenager was a difficult time, because I did not get along with anyone at that stage and anything that my mother had to say would frustrate me faster and further along, deeper than anyone else.

I do not quite know why that is; after all, they really do so much for us! They gave birth to us, stayed up with us when we were sick, and wiped away the tears when we had a fall. **(I have often considered the natural inclination to blame our mothers for things when they are usually the ones that do the most for us).**

Moms do such a good job at showing love and affection to us, that we start to take them for granted, because we know they will always love us. This, of course, is NOT the best way to behave—especially to someone you love! Unfortunately, though, it happens quite a bit. The fact is, that sometimes we give the worst treatment to the ones we love and that love us the most—those closest to us.

Conversely, you may have found that you were really perhaps NEVER able to bond with your mother and/or get really close to her. I have several friends that have experienced this kind of situation and it truly is the most difficult, because it follows you throughout your adult-life! You just sink when you acknowledge and know that you do not have the "closeness" that you truly desire and so much long for.

Many times, this lack of intimacy with your mother can lead to problems with eating disorders, substance, or drugs and alcohol abuse. Women start to seek out other things as replacements, just so they can "feel" better. With eating disorders, most are then merely looking for love and attention for the majority of the time. In most cases, it very well may have less, little, or nothing at all to do with the actual food itself.

Other times, they withhold food, such as in the case of anorexia, because they do not feel as though they are worthy of food, or should not be deserving or able to fully enjoy it at all. Then you have those cases where girls decide to over-compensate, by trying to be the best in school, their career, maybe sports or whatever they do, in order to try to win affection, or make themselves feel like they do not need anyone at all.

Of course, the truth is that we ALL need other people, and parents are fundamentally important to us, not only in how they raised us, but also in the love, kindness, and affection we get while growing up. This truly helps to shape our personalities and who we will become in our adult lives.

When I talk about the importance of getting along with women in our lives, I place heavy emphasis on our mothers, because the relationship with our mothers is truly important to a woman's life and well-being.

I want to offer some encouragement to you if you are reading this and feel that maybe you do not have the best relationship—the one that you desire with your mother.

The fact is that there are so many reasons why parents treat us a certain way while we are young and growing up. However, the most important thing for you to know is, that even if you were not shown the kind of love and affection that you wanted, I promise that you were and are still very much loved today!

If you feel deprived of a loving relationship from your mother, this most likely has to do with the way she was shown love and affection by her mother and even her father.

Perhaps she had a sibling that was favored, or she felt like she did not do things well enough to receive praise. She could have been abused verbally, physically and emotionally. All these things will contribute to how you were raised and if your mom did not seek help to work through these issues, then they are going to affect how she does things in her life. That, in turn, means how you get raised and then treated as an adult will also by extension, be affected.

I decided to talk about this openly and honestly, because as women, our relationship with our mothers can really influence how we feel about ourselves. There is a direct correlation, cause-effect type relationship at play here, of sorts.

After all, this book is about you discovering what you can do to be the best YOU CAN BE.

True ambition is about learning the keys and secrets that will help you develop into everything YOU have dreamed of.

Many times, it is extremely difficult to get your parents to talk about the challenges they had growing up. However, if you *do* know how they were raised, it will help you understand a little better, the things in your own life.

It helps learning about this, for you might very well connect the dots, to finally finding out about how and why you were or were not treated a certain way.

Sometimes, just realizing the reality that they had growing up, will help you have compassion for them, which then can lead to healing and forgiveness. It may not happen overnight but the goal for you is to heal yourself of those very things that may have hurt you.

Perhaps you were given everything that a child deserves. This could include all the love, affection, and attention from both parents. But you were a "problem" child and you have not forgiven yourself for things that you may have done while you were growing up.

Teenage years can be extremely volatile and thus also very difficult on the parents! REMEMBER: they only want the very best for you (even if/when it does not feel like it!).

Sometimes it takes years for you to understand that. Maybe they went about it all wrong, but they had good intentions. You are an adult now, so it may very well be the time to decide and opt to move on, putting the blame-game and finger pointing to rest.

Once you turn 18 years old, you are responsible for who you become and what you accomplish. Let us forgive and learn to develop the ultimate female relationship, the one with our mothers, to its fullest potential and capacity. Let go of any resentment, anger or hostile emotions.

If you are looking for a good way to rebuild a relationship with your mom, do it with loving-kindness and tender loving care (TLC). Here are some tips and suggestions:

Write her a letter, letting her know your side of things. Be open about things and situations that happened to you, that made you feel a certain way. Be sure to also include good things that she did for you, that made you feel good. Remind her that you love her and that a good relationship is important to you. Let her know all the things that are in your heart.

Yes, you are taking a chance here and you may not like the reaction that you may get, but this is important enough to take a chance on. IT IS A MUST!

As you begin to grow as a mature, self-confident woman, you need to deal with things that are not always pleasant –even things from your past.

So, let us get started then, by reaching out in love and trying to find common ground here! *(After all, she is the only mother you have)*.

On the other hand, if you are blessed and have a great relationship with your mom, then this is the perfect time to reach out to her and tell her again how amazing she is , as well as how your relationship has meant so much to you.

Always tell her how much you love and respect her for how she treated you and raised you. When and if YOU become a mother and experience the joys and sadness of mothering/motherhood, YOU too will see how much hard work is put into raising a child.

Moms, a lot of times, DO NOT get credit where credit is due, so take this opportunity to tell her what she means to you. Now let us look at what some women are doing to make money and create wealth for themselves

WOMEN AND WEALTH

Even though women are highly competitive, they can also celebrate and share in one-another's successes and heights. This is also true when talking about fortunes, profits and wealth. According to sources the top 10 wealthy women in the world are:

TOP 10 - World's Richest Women... (9 March 2006)... *Wealth in USD$*				
Name	Wealth	Source	Citizenship	Personal
Liliane Bettencourt	$16.0 b	L'Oreal	France	83yo – Married, 1 child
Christy Walton	$15.9 b	Wal-Mart	USA	51yo – Widowed, 1 child
Alice Walton	$15.7 b	(inheritance) Wal-Mart	USA	56yo – Divorced
Helen Walton	$15.6 b	Wal-Mart	USA	86yo – Widowed, 4 children
Abigail Johnson	$12.5 b	Fidelity investments	USA	44yo – Married, 2 children
Barbara Cox Anthony	$12.4 b	media/entertainment	USA	82yo – Married, 2 children
Anne Cox Chambers	$12.4 b	media/entertainment	USA	86yo – Divorced, 3 children
Jacqueline Mars	$10.0 b	candy (incl. Mars bar)	USA	66yo – Divorced, 3 children
Birgit Rausing & family	$8.6 b	Tetra Laval (packaging manufacture)	Sweden	82yo – Widowed, 3 children
Susanne Klatten	$8.1 b	BMW	Germany	43yo – Married, 3 children

Women own more than 47% of the stocks (Source: Peter Hart and NASD and the Investment Institute)

Women are projected to acquire over 85% of the $12 trillion growth of U.S. private wealth between 1995 and 2010 (Source: Marti Barletta of Trend-Sight Group)

Cheering each other on to reach and aspire even higher, more and more women embrace learning and education, to better and enrich themselves. This strategy serves them well on their paths to realizing their dreams, hopes and aspirations.

Education

Since 1984, the number of women in graduate schools has exceeded the number of men. (Source: National Center for Education Statistics, 1997)

Women received 238,563 of the Master's degrees conferred in 1996-1997, whereas men earned 181,062 of the Master' degrees conferred in 1996-97 (Source: Department of Education)

- Women Top-Ranked* Professional Schools

- Engineering 15%

- Business 30%

- Law 44%

- Medicine 45%

   Top-ranked schools by U.S. News and World Report

WHAT YOU SHOULD LEARN FROM THIS CHAPTER

Key-reminders and insights from Chapter 6 highlight:

- Although women are more likely to have **friendships based on emotion** rather than things that we have in common with other women, we are also more likely to **squabble amongst ourselves**.

- The **competitive nature of the world** we live and function in as women breaks down easily into traditionally male-dominated roles, domains and areas. This has led to an increasingly competitive nature in women, even and especially amongst themselves!

- It is important to **recognize how vital women are to each other**. We need other women in our lives –whether friends, mothers, sisters, etc—to help us get through our own issues, joys, and trials.

- **Self-esteem** is often at the heart of problems that we have in our **relationships with other women** as well as **our relationships with ourselves**. Building self-esteem is a critical step to being our BEST 'self', and achieving the MOST FULLFILLED relationships with others.

- Women are taking charge in every part of the "industry" of wealth, including education, top-paying jobs, investments, and just about every other field of career and/or finance. Set your aims high—your goals are ready to be achieved!

Chapter 7

Money Management that Makes Cents

"Happiness is not in the mere possession of money; it lies in the joy of achievement, in the thrill of creative effort."

—*Franklin D. Roosevelt*

F rom budgeting and saving, to investing and spending, financial decisions are about weighing your choices and making informed decisions.

Managing your money can seem confusing and overwhelming at first glance, but if you take it step-by-step, you can actually understand personal finance better than you ever thought possible.

For many of you reading this, you may already have a good handle on your finances. However, I know that there are many things about managing your money that all women should learn but that simply is not taught in school. This would include things like balancing your checkbook, investing, and other reasonable ways to make sure you are as financially comfortable as you can be.

It simply does not make sense for you to rely one someone (or anyone!) else—such as a boyfriend or husband—to take care of these matters. Sure, he may be in charge of the finances, but it is up to you to understand them as well, to ensure that you are a complete and whole person able to take care of herself (independently, when it matters!). My advice? Get wise, be smart, and take the time to learn all you can about finances!

Let us get into one of my favorite success stories about how this incredible brilliant writer hit it big!

A GREAT EXAMPLE: JOANNE (JK) ROWLING

Joanne Rowling is the famed author of the Harry Potter series of fantasy books under the pen name J.K. Rowling. She is not only a celebrity author, but she has also gained international attention, won multiple awards, and sold over three hundred million copies worldwide. In February 2004, Forbes magazine estimated her fortune at £576 million (just over US$1 billion), making her the first person ever to become a $US billionaire by writing books.

By December of 1994, Rowling was still mourning her mother who died four years earlier. She had just gone through a divorce and moved to Edinburgh, Scotland with her daughter, to be near her sister.

Unemployed and living on state benefits, she completed her first novel, doing some of the work in local Edinburgh cafés. In fact, it is rumored that she wrote in local cafés in order to escape from her unheated flat, but in a 2001 BBC interview,

Rowling remarked, "I am not stupid enough to rent an unheated flat in Edinburgh in midwinter. It had heating."

In 1995, Rowling completed her manuscript for *Harry Potter and the Philosopher's Stone*, on an old manual typewriter. Upon the enthusiastic response of Bryony Evans, a reader who had been asked to review the first three chapters of the book, the Fulham-based Christopher Little Literary Agents agreed to represent Rowling in her quest for a publisher. The book was handed to twelve publishing houses, all of which rejected it. A year later, she was finally given the green light (and a £1500 advance) by the editor Barry Cunningham, from the small publisher Bloomsbury.

Although Bloomsbury had agreed to publish the book, Cunningham claims he advised Rowling to get a day-job, as she had little chance of making money in children's books.

Soon after, Rowling received an £8000 grant from the Scottish Arts Council to enable her to continue writing. The following spring, an auction was held in the United States for the rights to publish the novel, and was won by Scholastic Inc, who paid Rowling more than $100,000. Rowling has said she "nearly died" when she heard the news.

In June 1997, Bloomsbury published Philosopher's Stone with an initial print run of only 1000 copies, 500 of which were distributed to libraries. Today, such copies are valued at between £16,000 and £25,000 each. The Queen has even honored Rowling by making her an Officer of the Order of the British Empire.

The last three volumes in the series have all been the fastest-selling books in history, grossing more in their opening 24 hours than blockbuster films. Book Six of her series earned The Guinness World Records Award, for being the fastest selling book ever. In June 2006, the British public named Rowling *"the greatest living British writer"*.

Harry Potter has made Rowling a well-known and a very successful author, but after Rowling finishes the final Harry Potter book, she plans to continue writing.

Rowling declared, in a recent interview, that she will most likely not use a pen-name, as the press would quickly discover her true identity.

In 2001, the UK fundraiser Comic Relief asked three bestselling British authors to submit booklets related to their most famous works for publication. For every pound raised, a pound would go towards combating poverty and social inequality across the globe. Rowling's two booklets, *Fantastic Beasts and Where to Find Them* and *Quidditch Through the Ages*, are ostensibly facsimiles of books found in the Hogwarts library, and are written under the names of their fictional authors, Newt Scamander and Kennilworthy Whisp. Since going on sale in March 2001, the books have raised £15.7 million ($30 million) for the fund. The £10.8 million ($20 million) raised outside the UK has been channeled into a newly created International Fund for Children and Young People in Crisis. She has also personally given £22 million to Comic Relief.

Rowling has contributed money and support to many other charitable causes, especially research and treatment of multiple sclerosis, from which her mother died in 1990. This death heavily affected her writing, according to Rowling. In 2006, Rowling contributed a substantial sum of money, towards the creation of a new Centre for Regenerative Medicine in Edinburgh.

In January 2006, Rowling went to Bucharest to raise funds for the Children's High Level Group, an organization devoted to enforcing the human rights of children, particularly in Eastern Europe. On August 1st and 2nd, 2006, she read alongside Stephen King and John Irving, at Radio City Music Hall in New York City. Profits from the event were donated to the Haven Foundation, a charity that aids actors left uninsurable and unable to work, and the medical NGO *Médecins Sans Frontières*.

J.K. Rowling is a tremendous example of how dedicating yourself to doing what you love, sticking to it with the right goals, and having the right management on your side, CAN help you to achieve all of your financial objectives. She also shows that money IS NOT everything! Though it does allow her quite a bit of freedom, she intends to continue writing—thus doing what she has always loved best. Furthermore, she has not forgotten to spread her good fortune by contributing to worthy causes.

BUDGETING

This is a word that most of us women hate to hear and think about (let alone doing it!). After all, who wants to live life with financial limitations? As unattractive as it might seem, though, it will serve you well to buy only what you can afford, not over-spend, or go into debt.

These fiscal discipline and good habits will ensure that your road to success is a much smoother one. If you choose to live beyond your means now, you will pay the price along the way with poor credit scores, lack of saving, debt, and STRESS!

We all have budgets—some may be larger with more spending freedom than some others—but even when you reach your financial goals, you still have to watch what you spend so that you do not lose your hard-earned money. No one wants to have to reduce the lifestyle they become accustomed to.

Furthermore, you will want to learn how to make that money work for you so it can grow into larger amounts, which will permit you to enjoy your life in the long run, help the ones that you love, and give to worthy causes.

If you want to make sure that you are not spending more than you are earning, you need to make a budget. A budget is a plan for your money that maps out how much you make (your income) and how much you spend (your expenses). The chart below offers some advice on how to divide and allocate your after-tax household income wisely.

Guideline for after-tax expenses:

- 30%: shelter

- 10%: fixed expenses

- 10%: loan payments

- 10%: personal spending

- 10%: savings

Four-step program

Step One: Add Up Your Income

To set up a monthly budget, you need to know how much money you have available to spend every month, after you pay your taxes. This is your **net household income**, because it is the number that is left AFTER you have paid out all your deductions to the government.

If you get paid once a month, just look on your pay stub to see your net monthly income.

If you get paid weekly, every two weeks or twice a month, you will need to do some math to figure out your net monthly income:

- For weekly pay, multiply the weekly amount by 4.333

- For every-two-week pay, multiply the amounts by 2.167

- For twice-a-month pay, multiply the amounts by 2

Step Two: Estimate Your Expenses

Here is where you write down what you think you will be spending your money on. It is easier to remember all the places your money goes if you divide your expenses into groups.

You can lump them into big groups, like "shelter" and "loans," or you can get really specific, and figure out how much you spend monthly on more particular things like "clothes" and "transportation." Divide your expenses up in whatever way is easiest for you to keep track of.

Step Three: Figure Out the Difference

After you have created your budget, you need to keep records of your actual monthly income and expenses. This will help you understand the difference between the amount you plan to spend on something, and the amount you actually spend. Save your receipts, so you can really know where your money is going. You would be surprised how much money gets spent on that daily latte.

You may be surprised to discover a lot of gaps between these two areas in the beginning. That is exactly why coming up with a budget is such a good idea. It shows how you really spend your money.

Step Four: Track, Trim, and Target

After you pay attention to your spending habits for a little while, you may realize that you are spending more money than you are actually making. You will also see where you are spending too much money.

In some cases, it is then also NOT too hard to cut expenses!

In others, though it is and can be very hard and challenging. For example, you have to pay your rent and electricity bill, but you do *not* have to buy a new pair of purple suede shoes with a *really* cute silver buckle. (and the "must have" handbag to match!)

Once you get used to only spending as much as you have coming in, you will probably feel much more relaxed. You will not feel the pressure of dealing with bills that you do not have the money to pay for.

And you might even have enough left over to treat yourself from time to time, or to save some money for the future.

SIDEBAR: When I was not making a lot of money early on, it meant more to me to have something saved in the bank, than a great pair of jeans. I would rather know I had something to fall back on.

You can always get jeans later, but sometimes you need that savings as a safety net when things happen that you were not expecting and when you are on your own, things always come up.

GOALS

Remember back in chapter 2 when we discussed identifying your goals and then going after them? Well, managing your money has a lot to do with making goals and then setting up a strategy for achieving them. Remember, write down everything you do to make it concrete and defined. It will increase your chances of succeeding many times over.

The only thing about money is that there are some obstacles involved that mean that you need to decide what things you *need*, like food, and a roof over your head, and things that you *want*, like a great car.

The Planning Process

Would you like to own your own home one-day? Would you like to buy a car? Everybody has a dream that requires money to help make it come true. The difference between those people who realize their dreams and those that do not is: that those who do have a plan. Here's a four-step model to help you make your dreams come true. Writing things down is the unstated rule of thumb, for this entire process.

Assess Needs—Your *wants* are things that may make your life easier or more enjoyable, but which you do not need to live. You may want a new plasma screen TV for your bedroom, for example, but you do not NEED one. You *do* need a winter coat, and a bed. Without these things, your life would be very difficult. Just make sure the coat you buy is not the really cute one that you will only use a few times a year because you live in sunny California near the beach! Opt for something that you can afford today, and remember that once you hit your financial goals, you can splurge on a hot coat and matching boots. It is all about your timing and if you really want those things, you will work smarter and harder to get them.

So make a list of everything that would be good to have in your life, and write it down. Next, divide the list. Go through every item, and mark it with a "W" (for want) or an "N" (for need).

If there is anything you are not sure of, ask yourself how your life would be improved if you had it (and how terrible it would be if you did not). This will help tell you whether it is a "want," or a "need." This part may be quite challenging, because it is easy to justify why you "need" pretty, impractical things. But be honest with what you can afford.

Set Goals—Put aside your "want" list. Now, turn your "need" list into a collection of goals. Some people like to set daily, weekly, and yearly goals for themselves. Set up your "goal list" in whatever way works best for you.

Make a Plan—With goals in hand, you must now begin to develop a plan for achieving them. Imagine yourself moving toward each goal. Break it down into steps. If you can afford to set aside $10 a week toward purchasing a winter coat, for example, figure out how long it will take before you have enough money to buy it. Then make a calendar with an instruction to save $10 a week. Remember, writing your plan down makes it easier to achieve. I cannot say this enough.

Take Action—Now you have a plan. Congratulations! Print several copies, look at them often, and take action.

Get S.M.A.R.T.

A realistic goal is SMART (in more ways than one):

- **S**pecific

- **M**easurable

- **A**ttainable

- **R**elevant

- **T**ime-related

SPECIFIC: Smart goals are specific enough to move a person into action. For example, deciding to save enough money to buy a refrigerator (as opposed to simply saying, "Save some money.")

MEASURABLE: You need to know when you have reached your goal, or how close you are to it. Goals which aren't measurable, like "I would just like to have more money," are much harder to achieve. What's more, there is no way to tell when you have gotten there. For example, a refrigerator costs $600, and you have $300 already saved. You need $300 more before you can buy the refrigerator.

ATTAINABLE: The steps toward reaching your goal need to be possible. For example, my budget must allow me to put aside enough money each week in order for me to meet my goal within one year.

RELEVANT: The goal needs to make sense. You do not want to work toward a goal that does not fit your needs. For example, you do not need to save money for eighteen pairs of shoes!

TIME-RELATED: It is important to set a definite target date. For example, the repairman says my refrigerator will not last another year. Therefore, I need to get my new refrigerator in the next eight months.

Balancing Your Checkbook

It is important to keep track of all the activities in your account in your check register (the little notebook that comes with your checks). This keeps you organized, allows you to monitor your own financial activities more actively, and lets you spot every single inaccuracy that pops up from bank calculations—you may be surprised at how common they really are!

Here's how:

- **Step 1**: Get a clean piece of paper and list the current balance from your bank statement.

- **Step 2**: Add any deposits that you have recorded in your check register, but that are not yet shown on the statement.

- **Step 3**: Subtract any outstanding checks, withdrawals you have made with your debit card, regular automatic payments you set up, and any withdrawals you make at a bank machine.

- **Step 4:** Compare the result you arrive at with the balance in your check register. NOTE: The balance in your check register should be adjusted to include: (a) deductions for service fees or other charges; (b) additions for direct deposits and interest earned.

Saving

Saving money is something most of us want to do, but it is also something we do not always do. Saving is easier than you think, as long as you know what you are doing with the basics of savings and what interest can do for you.

Interest calculations

Simple Interest Calculation—With the simple interest calculation, interest is calculated on the original amount of your deposit, year after year.

The formula is:

Original dollar amount x Interest rate x Length of time (in years) = Amount earned

EXAMPLE: If you had $100 in a savings account that paid 2% per year simple interest, you would earn $2 in interest by the end of the first year.

$$\$100 \times 0.02 \times 1 = \$2$$

At the end of two years, you would have earned $4. The account would continue to grow at a rate of $2 per year, despite the fact that, at the end of the first year you had $102 in the account.

Compound Interest Calculation

With the compound interest calculation, interest is paid on the original amount of the deposit, plus any interest earned.

The formula is:

(Original dollar amount + Earned interest) x Interest rate x Length of time = Amount earned

EXAMPLE: If you had $100 in a savings account that paid 2% interest compounded annually, the first year you would earn $2 in interest. The calculation the first year would look like this:

$$\$100 \times 0.02 \times 1 = \$2 \text{ (interest for the first year)}$$
$$\$100 + \$2 = \$102 \text{ (total amount in account at the end of the year)}$$

With compound interest, at the end of the second year you would earn $2.04 in interest—more than the first year, because the interest would be calculated on your new total of $102, and not just on your original deposit as it did in the simple interest example. By the end of the third year, you would have earned $6.12 in total interest. The calculations for the second and third years look like this:

Second year: $102 x 0.02 x 1 = 2.04

(Interest earned at the end of the second year)

Third year: $104.04 x 0.02 x 1 = 2.08
(Interest earned at the end of the third year)

$104.04 + 2.08 = 106.12
(Total amount in account at the end of the third year)

The Rule of 72

Sometimes, it helps to remember simple mathematical rules when you are working toward saving for a certain goal. Here is one, called "the rule of 72."

The "Rule of 72" helps to figure out how many years it will take to double your money. Here, you divide 72 by the rate of interest you're getting. The answer will tell you the number of years it will take you to double your original deposit, no matter how much it is.

72 ÷ Interest rate = Years to double investment

For example, it will take you 28.8 years to double your money at an interest rate of 2.5% per year.

You can also use the "Rule of 72" to figure out what interest rate you need to double your money in a set amount of years.

72 ÷ Years to double investment= Interest rate required

For example, this calculation will tell you that you need to get an interest rate of 7.2% per year if you want to double your money in 10 years.

Credit Cards

At some point in our lives, most of us borrow money. Even if you do not have a mortgage or a car loan, you are still borrowing money if you use a credit card.

In fact, credit cards are one of the most common forms of borrowing money. For example, with credit cards, consumers can make purchases and can delay having to pay these purchases off.

Because it is a convenience, they pay interest to the financial institution that issued them the card if the balance is not fully paid off each month.

Credit Cards 101

Credit cards have advantages, and when used wisely, can be an indispensable financial management tool.

Owning a credit card comes with many advantages. Credit cards give you the ability to buy needed items immediately, and they also allow you to get an "interest-free" loan, as long as you pay your balance in full by the due date.

Credit cards also act as a safety net in case you need emergency funds, they are more convenient than writing checks, offer reward points which you can redeem for products or services, and allow you to buy products or services over the Internet or phone.

Credit cards also make traveling easier by providing you with local currency when traveling, and because they are accepted almost everywhere you go around the world. And finally, credit cards offer you an extra level of protection through zero liability policies. While credit cards offer convenience and reliability, there are things one should keep in mind when using a credit card.

While credit cards offer interest-free loans to those who pay off their entire balance every month, those who do not will have to incur some interest charges. And, if not managed properly, credit card use can sometimes get out of hand, so make sure that you use your credit wisely. Also, keep in mind that often, interest on cash advances made on credit cards are counted from the day the cash advance is taken. And please, do not give your boyfriend your credit card to use; nor should you have a joint account card with his name. We will talk more about this in our highly anticipated chapter on Meeting and Keeping Mr. Right.

Choosing a Card

Is it a convenience? Many consumers choose to pay their credit cards in full each month. This is the best way to know what you are spending and it will keep you on top of your bills. Plus, you will be earning a great credit rating because you pay in full and on time. A great credit rating is certainly something to strive for. You will save money in the future when you want to buy a house, car, or anything that requires a loan where the lenders will look at your credit report.

Many people also use credit cards because it is easier to pay with a credit card than to worry about having enough cash on hand. For these people, the card's interest rate is probably not too important. *(More important is probably the size of the annual fee and the card's special features!)*

Do you plan ahead? Some credit cards offer a low rate for the first few months. These can be a good choice for people who plan to make a large purchase and pay for it quickly. But you must stick to this plan, because interest rates on these cards are usually only low for a set and brief amount of time.

Do you plan to maintain a balance? Some credit card users do not pay off their credit card balances every month. If you plan to keep a balance, it is important to shop for the card with the lowest rate. This way, you will cut down on the amount of interest you have to pay every month. But if your average balance is less than $1,000, watch out for the annual fee!

Sometimes, a credit card's annual fee could cost more than what you would have paid in interest on a higher-interest card. If you plan to keep your balance small, look for a card that has no annual fee with the lowest interest rate you can find.

Credit Costs!

When you use your credit card you are, in effect, taking out a loan for your purchases from your financial institution. In return for this, the bank may charge you interest, or other fees, such as an annual fee.

If you always pay the amount owing on your credit card by the payment due date, you never have to pay interest.

If you do not pay the amount owing on your credit card in full by the due date, the interest you are charged will depend on whether the balance on your card is a new purchase, something you bought in the past and never paid off, a cash advance, or a balance transfer.

Pay attention to what you are purchasing, and remember you are in the building phase of your financial life. So stay focused on the goal of getting ahead, and avoiding getting behind on bills and credit cards.

The Power of $50 a Month

Even though you do not always have to pay off the entire balance on your credit card every month, you do need to pay something. This is called the "minimum payment." Sometimes people do not realize how long it will take them to pay off their debt if they pay only this every month. If you can afford to pay a little bit more than the minimum payment every month—say, $50 extra—it can make a big difference to how quickly you can pay off your whole debt.

Debt

Debt load is a term that is used to describe how much debt a person has. It is often used to understand if you are carrying a "safe" or reasonable amount of debt. Creditors look at how much debt you have, compared to how much income you have. This is called a debt/income ratio. The debt/income ratio is calculated monthly. It shows creditors how good, or bad, your financial health is.

You can figure out this ratio by adding up all of your monthly payments except for those that have to do with housing, utilities or taxes. This is your monthly debt.

Next, divide your total gross (before any deductions are made) annual income by twelve to get your gross monthly income. Then divide your monthly debt by your gross monthly income. This is your monthly non-housing debt/income ratio. It is usually expressed as a percentage, so move the decimal point two places to the right.

RULE OF THUMB—If your non-housing debt is 10% of your income or less, you're in great financial shape. If your non-housing debt is between 10% and 20%, then you will probably be able to get credit. But the closer you get to 20%, the closer you get to the edge of a reasonable debt load.

What are you worth?

Assets are things that you own. Even if you still owe money on them, they are assets. These can be things like your car, house, entertainment system, patio furniture, and jewelry. Your list of assets also includes the contents of your bank accounts; cash in your wallet, and investments.

To figure out your total assets, you have to know how much everything on your list is worth. Consider what you could expect to sell something for—and be honest with your guesses. Remember that when you are making your purchases, it is key to understand the real value for the items that you are buying.

For example, if you are buying your first car, it may be in your best interest to consider a pre-owned car *versus* the new one that will lose twenty percent of its value once you drive it out of the showroom.

If you are purchasing real estate, pay attention to the market. Are you buying at the right time? Is the market high? If so, will you be over-paying? Is the market slowing down? In this case you may decide to wait a little longer to see where things go, and where the interest rate is headed.

Your home is likely the largest purchase you will ever make, so you will want to make sure that you get a good deal. This is important so that when you decide to sell it, you will have achieved a favorable amount of equity.

If you buy when the market is high, chances are the market will correct itself.

This means that you risk making only a slim amount of money, breaking even, or even losing money when you decide to sell it. Learn to pay attention to issues such as the interest rate, and buy when things make sense.

DO NOT just buy because you want it and you are trying to desperately compete with your group of friends! It is better to start small and work your way up. There will be a day when you get everything you want. After all, that is what this book is all about! Having it all—how to get it, and how to keep it!

Liabilities are what you owe, including finance charges. For example, your liability is not the cost of your car, but the total amount of the car loan to be repaid—including interest. You can figure this out by multiplying the payment amount, by the number of payments left to pay off the loan.

Ideally, your list of assets will be worth more than your list of liabilities. If it is not, remember that that this is a snapshot in time. Everything—your assets and liabilities—may very well always be changing.

Borrowing

When you think about borrowing money, there are several things to consider. You should be able to:

Identify different sources and institutions that lend money

Understand the descriptions of the available loans

Know how to calculate the cost of credit

Figure out your own debt limit

Most consumer credit comes from: *banks, trust companies, finance companies, and other lending institutions.* In addition, many people borrow from relatives or other individuals. Wherever you borrow from, be sure to get a signed contract, and READ THE FINE PRINT.

It is very hard to admit when you are having a problem with debt. It can feel uncomfortable to admit that you did not plan your spending well. Here are some signs that might indicate that you are headed for trouble:

- Next month's bills arrive before you have paid the ones from last month

- You do not know how much you owe

- You get a new loan to pay old loans

- You only pay the minimum amount due each month

- You spend more than 20% of your net income (after paying rent or mortgage) on your debts

- You are using your savings to pay for day-today expenses

- There are more bills than you thought

- You know what past-due notices look like

- You get an overdue balance on a credit card statement

- You avoid opening letters

- You rarely keep a running balance in your checkbook

Getting Out of Debt

There are two great ways to change your debt load and debt/income ratio: cut spending and bring in more money.

Cutting spending can be the fastest way to reduce debt load, unless additional work and income are readily available. Think of it as surgery for your money management. But as you heal with better financial health, you will probably also notice that your attitude, relations with others, emotions, and sense of humor improve too.

You do not have to keep adding to your debt load by continuing to buy stuff. Remember, you may have found a terrific bargain on a new surround-sound stereo system for your home entertainment area, but if you do not pay it off for three years, the money you "saved" will not matter.

Avoid impulse purchases. These are the things you pick up at the cash register that you had no intention of buying when you entered the store. You would be surprised at what a difference this can make. Stay away from the mall when you are on your lunch break. Do not tell yourself that you are just browsing; this is the quickest way to walk out with that alluring new fragrance you do not need.

If you go out to lunch with a friend, share something. The meals we get served today are more than enough to share. Besides, it will help your waistline! Let your good friends know that you are saving money and that you would rather have them come over to your house for dinner, than go out to a restaurant.

Even better, each person can bring something different, and you can rent a movie together. You will spend more time laughing, and you will have a much better time than you would at a snooty restaurant. Plus, going out to eat always seems to involve way more calories and cocktails then we need. Do you NOT agree?

If you do not know how to cook, this is something that you should learn. Watch the cooking channel and take notes, or go online and pull up your favorite meal. You can get great recipes online. Then you can cook, or take your lunch to work. Compare the difference between the expense of lunch at a restaurant for a week and a week of lunches brought from home. The difference may surprise you.

Just one of these changes will give you a great start to improving your financial life. And your future husband will thank you. Every man loves a great home-cooked meal.

Think about ways to bring in additional money: either a part-time job or a better paying primary job. A second job could include doing some secretarial work on weekends for a good friend that really needs the help. It does not always mean getting hired by another employer. Think about things you can do from your home that will help you add extra income.

Talking to Bill Collectors

Talk sooner than later. Do not wait for a bill collector to call you. When you are in financial trouble, it is very important to talk to your creditors as soon as possible. Why? Because your creditors might be charging you more in the mean time.

You would also be taken more seriously by addressing your financial difficulties immediately, rather than ignoring them.

The bill collector's job is to ask you to pay everything you owe as soon as possible. With that in mind, follow these tips:

- Do not lose your temper

- If it is a bad time, get the collector's number, make an appointment and call back

- Be prepared with the details of how much you owe

- Keep your worksheet information by the phone so you can talk intelligently

- Be ready to suggest a plan for dealing with your debt

- Listen to the suggestions of the bill collector

- If you are having trouble with one bill collector, ask for another

Your Rights

Debt does not give your creditors license to pester you. They must behave according to certain rules.

Debt collectors are required to:

- Inform you, in writing, of the amount of your debt and the name of the creditor

- Give you information about your right to dispute the debt

- Give you written proof of the debt if you dispute it

Money is not always an easy topic. In fact, for most people, it is one of the largest concerns in their lives. As long as you learn and practice proper money management, however, you will ensure that you are much better off. You will also be able to keep your goals on track, and your achievements in sight!

WHAT YOU SHOULD LEARN
FROM THIS CHAPTER

Key-reminders and insights from Chapter 7 highlight:

- You can take control of your financial situation, no matter what your income situation may be.

- Budgeting is a major part of your ability to obtain financial stability, as well as a great way to plan for your future and your goals.

- Debt is a serious issue, and should be dealt with now. There are many ways to deal with debt, and there are lots of different services out there to help you to decrease or remove your debt while maintaining the best possible credit score that you can achieve.

- The most important part of your money is to know your rights— what you can and cannot do, and what can or cannot be done to you.

Chapter 8

Finding Mr. Right and Keeping Him

"True love does not come by finding the perfect person, but by learning to see an imperfect person perfectly."

—Jason Jordan

It goes without saying, that we are in a time when it seems like everyone is single and currently looking for the perfect partner. If you are a single woman, then you understand how frustrating the process can be to find Mr. Right when you may have even convinced yourself by now that he doesn't exit. You tell yourself that the only people that seem to have it made are the Barbie-dolls of the world and those with money and power.

Well, let me dispel that myth right now, because we all know that Hollywood is filled with beautiful lonely starlets that cannot seem to keep a husband, or even find true love themselves.

So, you inevitably ask, yourself: *If they can't find Mr. Right how can I?*

Let us all then just take a minute to read about a little girl that grew up to find her Prince Charming.

A GREAT EXAMPLE: FAITH HILL

Faith Perry was born in Jackson, Mississippi, but raised in the nearby town of Star. She began singing at a very early age. After briefly attending college, she moved to Nashville to attempt launching her singing career.

Faith's voice caught the attention of Warner Brothers Records executives, who eagerly gave her a record-deal. During this time, she married Dan Hill, an executive and songwriter, to whom she remained wed between 1988 and 1994.

Unfortunately, this relationship came to an end, but she kept her strength and life together. Shortly after being signed to Warner, Hill was given the opportunity to open for fellow country superstar Tim McGraw. You just never know when fate is going to bring you at the door to your opportunities and in Faith's case that is exactly what happened.

Hill began the Spontaneous Combustion Tour with country singer Tim McGraw and later started seeing him, breaking off her engagement to her former producer, Scott Hendricks. When McGraw proposed marriage to her in one of his tour trailers, he had to go perform right then, so she took a permanent marker and wrote her answer on the mirror. Hill, after touring with McGraw, married him on October 6, 1996. They have three daughters together: Gracie Katherine (b. 1997), Maggie Elizabeth (b. 1998) and Audrey Caroline (b. 2001).

The year 2000 was also very successful in a concert setting, as Hill and Tim McGraw staged the joint Soul2Soul Tour, one of the best-grossing concert tours of 2000. In April 2006, Hill and husband Tim McGraw embarked on their Soul2Soul II Tour 2006, which stands as the highest grossing country music tour to date, with a gross of $89 million.

Faith was not just blessed by a lot of luck. She worked hard to achieve her goals, and lived her life to the fullest, meeting lots of people. It is therefore no accident that she met Tim McGraw, the man who is perfect for her, and who she can love both romantically, and as a terrific person to work with!

Understand that you do not always get it right the first time. Sure, we all have dreams of the perfect wedding, honeymoon, and all the great things that follow, but life throws challenges and sometimes you make the wrong choice.

If you continue to get back up when you are knocked down, you will start to win and the knowledge that you will have gained, having gone through difficult times, can serve you as the greatest life-lesson. It will be helping you along the way, to stay away from repeating these patterns, mistakes and choices to hopefully next time, (every time!) KNOW the right course for your life!

MEETING YOUR MR. RIGHT

I know many of my single friends talk openly about the frustration they have in this arena of life and on this topic. Many of them are online dating.

Let us talk about this for but a quick moment. It all seems to be the same scenario—you find yourself secretly wishing that this could be " the one", then you meet for coffee and you begin to share your stories of why you are single. You talk about your ex and what went wrong. He may tell you the same thing and then you ask about how much time they have been doing the internet dating thing? Does this sound familiar?

One of my dear friends tells me "I get sick and tired of hearing myself tell the same story. It is like I know what they are all going to ask. All I am thinking when I meet them is if they are semi-good looking and interesting. Then I start pondering: I wonder how many girls this guy has slept with online?"

She also mentions constantly that she does not know how much to trust them if she does decide to move forward with a guy she has met online. It really is the issue of trust and security that is so much more relevant when it comes to the internet and online dating.

Another problem about the "online thing" is that besides lying about their height, age and weight! you also cannot know for sure, if the guys you eventually agree to meet with are actually married! Then again, this is also true when you meet a guy in person. You never know if the guy you just met in the supermarket, or at a bar, has his wedding ring tucked into his wallet.

Therefore, you should be wary of any "exaggerations" that you see about a man's description on a dating website when compared to reality. Do not lose hope, though, because trust me, there are plenty of great guys out there that are looking for a wonderful committed relationship!

The important thing is to keep your wits about you, and not be too instantly trusting. Be true to yourself, embracing the opportunity, but also not being cold and uncaring at the same time. It is a delicate, fragile, and careful balance.

Here is where YOU come in! Listen to your instincts on how to get their attention and, of course, keep it.

Call me old-fashioned, but I still think the best way to meet your Mr. Right, is being out and about "living". Think about when you go to the store: how do you look? I am sure most of you do not really think about going to the store with your hair and make up done, looking good, but guess what? Perhaps you *should* begin to think about it! It matters!

Take advantage of all of the opportunities that you could have been overlooking until now. Did you know that grocery stores are one of the most popular places that guys go to meet women? It is practical, effective and it makes sense (at least from their point of view!) You may not know this, but lots of single guys peruse the fruit and veggie section looking for something more then just a ripe tomato.

Single men have to go to the grocery store too and when they do, trust me, they will sashay up and down the aisles looking for the " catch of the day" and I am NOT talking salmon here, ladies!

When you are out living, whether you are at the bookstore—which is another favorite place men like to go—**you need to look and be attractive**.

I am not saying that you need to strut in trying to look like Pamela Anderson— not at all—but you should always take pride in the way you look. DO NOT SKIMP ON YOURSELF! Do not just throw on an old tracksuit. Wear jeans that fit well and nice shoes. If they are open-toe shoes, make sure you have a nice pedicure, because a lot of men will check out your toes. Lots of men love feet, which includes not only your feet and toes, but also the shoes you wear.

Men love sexy feet and the most important thing for you to understand is that men are "turned on" visually. That is why they will always and forever take a peak at a pretty woman when she walks by. That is how they are wired; love it or hate it that is the simple truth. So with that knowledge, you need to understand that looking your best as often as possible, will only help your game.

It is important to know what looks good on you. No matter your shape or size, there is a type of outfit that looks great on you—it is all a matter of finding the right style to suit you.

Know how to dress so YOU look your best! Above all, please remember we all love those cute and sexy "Juicy" sweat suits, but just because they make it in your size, **does not mean that you should wear it outside the house.**

Make sure that you highlight the positive things about your body and understate the things that you feel make you uncomfortable. No matter how you look, though, skin-tight fit should never even be an option! It only accentuates the negative, and does little for the positive. Women get mad because they feel that all men care about is the way they look... well, guess what? It is partly true!

Let me explain: they want a woman that they find attractive, that is self confident, one that has her life together and on track. Men will run away FAST, if they feel that you are emotionally needy and need "rescuing".

They DO NOT want someone that eats badly and is gaining weight and does not take care of herself or tends to have a lack of concern for her own hygiene. They also do not want someone with loads of debt and bad credit. *Would you?*

Today women are better then ever and they work hard to have it all, so the competition is fierce. Make a decision that you are going to be the best you can be... BOTH in your health and the way that you look! If YOU feel good, you will hold your head high and your confidence will soar. Maybe you need to make a change; get a makeover change and update the way you wear your make up.

Just like fashion trends change, so do hair and make-up, so if you are wearing the same color eyeliner that you wore in college it's time to create a new fresh look. You will feel sexy and youthful. When you exude that kind of feeling, your body sends off a signal that men cannot ignore.

Because I have been a model, people just assume that naturally I do not have anything to worry about and that I effortlessly look good all the time. The truth is, that it takes a lot of effort to look good. I mean this in a positive way.

I personally put a lot of time and energy into presenting myself in a certain way. It would be fantastic if we could all pass out the magic pill for being a perfect 10 without having to do anything, except get the glass of water to drink it down with. But that is, unfortunately, NOT the way it works. If you want to look great, you must take action and you cannot be lazy! That is the bottom-line!

I work out at least 4 days week (usually 5) for an hour at a time. I make sure that I get lots of Cardio and I do kickboxing. My good friend teaches the class; her name is Renee and she has an incredible body. Unlike me, she is a mother of three

BEAUTIFUL AMBITION **153**

beautiful children and she does not look like she has had even one. The reason is hard work and discipline.

She keeps me fit several days a week doing kickboxing, *(which I highly recommend as one of the best over all exercises women can do)*. It will keep everything small and hard and you will look amazingly lean and defined. What more could you want?

The key is you have to work out and get some physical activity going on a consistent basis, no matter which 'type' you prefer or finally choose to stick to.

You must motivate yourself to move and work hard to get in shape. If you say, "I do not like to work out"—well, most people do not—you are overlooking the fact, that you do need it. Your physical health and mental stamina depend on it... not to mention getting into the latest tight, sexy "It" jeans that all the hot girls are wearing!

Watch your diet, too. This will be discussed in further detail in the next chapter. I will really talk about health food, diet and working out, but just know that this is one area that is non-negotiable. You must do it!

You also do not have to be a size 2. Be the best and healthiest size that works for you, and make sure that you feel happy in your size. Do not let others dictate that for you. Also, do not let yourself settle for less than you can be. We always have room for improvement in all areas of life, including our physique!

There are lots of ways to look great without breaking the bank and this will mean a little extra work for you, because you will most likely have to do it yourself. This might be true for such things as manicures, pedicures, facials and waxing. If you can afford these treatments, then consider yourself blessed. If you can't, do not worry or fuss about it. You will again at some point. For now though, you can and must learn to do it yourself, so relax and enjoy the process (even though it may not always be quite so easy to enjoy the waxing bit!).

Pick one or two nights a week that you can set aside and allow to pamper yourself. You really will feel great when you take pride in your body and appearance. Remember, men also love and appreciate it!

Go through your closet and deliberately get rid of things that do not fit you right, or are all worn out or completely outdated. If you can afford to go shopping, then spend your money on classic pieces that will go the distance throughout the new season... and maybe even the next one.

Invest in a few special pieces like a great winter coat, a killer pair of boots and a classic handbag. Then buy things that you can wear and mix-and-match all season long. If you are on a tighter budget, then shop at the high-end consignment stores. There are lots of them around that carry great clothes and many of them are almost new. You can pick up great accessories there as well.

Take care of the things you buy so that they will last you as long as you need them. Then you can always share them with the next person by bringing them back to the consignment stores when you are done with them. They might be another person's treasure!

Use this money you get when you bring them back, to find something new and wonderful that you might have been eyeing. Just like you have to have an action- plan to reach your dreams, you need an action-plan to look great and meet Mr. Right. That is the way it goes! So, get into the game and most importantly, try to have fun with it... you will NOT regret it!

If you take the time to start looking your best, you will get into it and begin to enjoy the process ever more. It will become a personal challenge and pleasure. Now you are probably saying to yourself "I have to look good for work all the time, so I just want to relax when I am off. I don't want to have to worry about my hair and make up". If this is the way you feel, my response would be this: While you don't need to dress up as though you are headed out somewhere formal, you should look clean, well-groomed, and attractive. It does not take much to put on just a bit of makeup, put your hair in a simple, yet flattering style, and wear something other than running shoes when you are outside of your home. After all, your shopping style has not done much for you yet, why not give the tried-and-true method a go?

I am here to help you and I want to be honest about this topic. I also want to make it clear to you that I am in no way suggesting that you need to be a perfect size 2 or 4! NOT AT ALL! Please understand that each of us has an ideal body type and size and some of us may very well NOT be able to maintain that weight and still feel energy to work, work out, take care of friends, and maybe you have children that you need to care for. You need to be a "healthy" weight FOR YOU! Since we are all created differently, you will know what works for you.

The average size of most American women is between a 10 and a 12. So work hard at it, but DO NOT under any circumstances begin any type of crazy dieting or (unsafe) unhealthy habits that can contribute to poor health in the long run.

The real idea here is to get you moving and feeling fit, healthy, confident and strong physically, emotionally and mentally.

There are no short cuts! That is the long and short of it. Just create a plan that works, that you can live with. Please remember this: You are not in competition with the Hollywood A list celebrities. They have loads of money at their disposal as well as assistants, personal trainers, chefs, and all kinds of things that help them stay in the best shape possible. Also, they are in fact 'paid' and have a vested interest to have that kind of look and discipline! It is part of their job!

But YOU are NOT them and although it is fun to watch them and you may have your favorites, under NO CIRCUMSTANCES put that kind of pressure on yourself! We are going after the perfect YOU. YOU are NOT trying to be some Celebrity. With that being said let's move right along to finding Mr. Right!

What to Expect When You Find Mr. Right

Just like you are not perfect, neither will Mr. Right be perfection either! The trick here is to find someone whose imperfections complement your own (that you can both live with!). Find somebody that you feel has perfections that far

156 CHAPTER EIGHT *Finding Mr. Right and Keeping Him*

outweigh the little quirks and differences. *(After all, that is and will be what makes him special, both for now and for later, right?)*

Among the most common things that women complain about and struggle with when they find a potential Mr. Right, is *(as I mentioned, before in this chapter and I will mention again)*, **the roving eye.**

It goes without saying that men are physical beings, and yes, they will forever love looking at beautiful sexy women. I do not care if you are married or single, guys will forever look. That is the reality.

And let us be brutally honest here: can you blame them? Women are gorgeous, and if someone is attractive enough that *you* would notice her, can you blame a man for doing the same? The guy is not dead and if he cannot appreciate another woman's beauty, then he will not be in a position to appreciate yours either!

Here is how you have to look at it. Looking is not wrong—it is lusting that will get him (and others potentially), into BIG TROUBLE. So whenever your guy takes a look at an attractive woman—without taking any additional actions, of course—you DO NOT simply have to make some or other catty or demeaning comment.

After all, then you will in the end just be seemingly jealous and possessive. You will end up coming across as a woman-hater with a very low self-esteem. Whatever you do, DO NOT make some snippy comment like: *"Can you believe that girl is wearing that slutty outfit?"* Most likely he likes—or at least doesn't mind—the dress she has on, though he will never tell you that. To him, this remark not only tells him that you are insecure, but it also lets him know that he does not need to be expecting you in something like that soon (to his dismay!). Even if you would NEVER (heaven forbid) wear something like that in a million years, he still likes to fantasize! REMEMBER that, and use it to your advantage.

What men do not understand is that all women are the jealous type (instinctively). It simply and really is in our very nature as females to be that way. However, we are also in control of our thoughts. That said, we can control, ignore, smile, and move on with the conversation as well.

It is also quite nice and mature, to compliment another woman when you think she is beautiful. You can tell her directly that she is beautiful for a change. Why NOT make her day? Does it not make you feel good when a woman tells you that she likes your purse, or that you look good in the sweater you are wearing? It is a very kind and confident move for you and your guy will find it sexy in turn. Take my word for it.

If your new man is taking a peak, let him off the hook and let it roll if he makes a comment that makes you feel insecure or hurts your feelings. It is up to you to understand that this is not necessarily about Mr. Right (or not!)

Ensure that you DO NOT simply excuse or settle for bad behavior because you think that you will NOT find someone else. Know what you are worth and your man will treat you accordingly. If he does not, simply move on!

You have to learn to let things roll and slide a little bit.

The Way Men Perceive Beauty

A lot of women feel that they fall short of the "Ideal Beauty" that they think men are looking for. First off, you need to know that men will be attracted to you and stay with you forever IF you make them feel good about themselves when they are with you. That is the real secret and key to success here.

If you nag, whine, and complain, he is not going to want to be around you. If you are needy and not self-sufficient he is not going to want to sweep you off your feet. Not all men want the Barbie-doll—and the ones that do, are likely not good matches for you anyway.

The fact is, just as much as they want a woman that is sweet, kind, fun, and nice—you too want the same characteristics from them! What a revelation and inspired thought!

You certainly DO NOT want to be dating an unattractive guy! This does not in turn, however, mean that you necessarily realistically want a Greek God either.

You want someone that takes pride in the way he looks and carries himself with confidence, not arrogance.

Men want a woman who smiles and looks like she is happy. That is a big turn-on for them. They like a women who has her life in order and together. Men are not looking to rescue someone; they want a partner. Dating today is different, because so many men are used to working with women on the job, they now expect women to make a similar income.

If you have a bit of money in the bank, a credit card, and especially if you own your own home (though rentals are not forbidden, of course!), you are and will find yourself, at the top of the list. Also, do not forget that not every guy out there is looking for a "super model". Men can find it very challenging to be with a woman if she is *too* good-looking. It takes a lot of confidence on their part to believe they will be able to make this 'ideal' looker-of-a-woman happy. So many times, they decide early on already that they are going to focus on what they find sexy and appealing and NOT just try to get the hottest girl they can.

After all, men are also looking to be treated right and they to want to make a relationship last. Women that seem "too perfect" can scare them. Instead, they decide to look for things that they really like, for example, a great smile and killer curves, or long beautiful hair and pretty eyes.

Maybe you have great legs. Guys know what they like and many times they go for women who are completely the opposite of what you would consider the "Ideal Beauty". That is also however, the whole case-in-point.

There is a guy out there right now waiting to sweep you off your feet. You just need to be the best "YOU" that you can be! Then start taking all these points and put them into action. By doing so, YOU too will have the pick of the litter and have them eating from your hands (proverbially speaking)!

You can make yourself crazy thinking about all the new requirements for finding Mr. Right, but do not forget to take a step back and remember that if you are practicing the things in this book, you are already ahead in your game. It is a balancing act to have it all together and you will fall short some of the times.

This is all just part of life! However you can start over the next day and get right back on track. That is the beauty of 'tomorrow'. If you decide that you are going to follow the program that is designed in this book in order to help YOU take your life to the next level, then YOU, TOO, can start hitting your goals and living your dream. You will not have to look too long for Mr. Right; after all, he is already looking for you!

When you are thriving and the world is your oyster, men will be much more available and attracted to you because they will feel good being around you.

SIDEBAR: I think about the time when I met my husband, for example. I was 22 years old at the time, working as a model. Thinking back on it now, I had so much on my plate when I met him… Yes, I was very attracted to him, but at the same time he scared me, because I thought that I would lose focus of my career if I dared getting involved! I did not want to give up anything that I had worked so hard to achieve up to this point. I did not want to derail myself from my plan to achieve my goals. I was still very young, and I had a lot of dreams that I intended to realize.

However, it was when I was getting my own life in gear and not even looking for Mr. Right, that Mr. Right came to *me*. Now you may say to yourself, "Tara, you were so young. What were you thinking?" Well, my situation was very different. First of all, my husband is 11 years older than me, which worked out well because I have always felt more comfortable with people older than myself. Furthermore, he had all of the qualities that I wanted, so I did not want to let something like fear make me pass up the man who could potentially be "the one" (and he *is* the one!).

He is handsome, charming, and very successful, yet self-made, which I find very sexy and appealing. He worked hard for his success and that turned me on.

He also treated me like a princess. So in my case, I had to decide whether I was going to let fear cause me to sabotage our relationship, or if I should look fear in the eyes and take a leap of faith. I took that leap, and it has been almost thirteen years of marital "bliss". We also share the same faith which has kept our lives balanced and on track.

We are partners in everything we do. We laugh, have a great time with each other, and, of course, he is my best friend. However, I also have a life with our children, my girl friends, and the professional projects that I still like to tackle.

When I told Jason that I really wanted to write this book for younger women, in order to help and empower them to reach their full potential and dreams, he was completely supportive.

There have been times that I have been afraid, but he kept me on track, reminding me of my passion and commitment to be my 'best' self, and give my utmost and best in everything that I do.

When you find YOUR Mr. Right, it is especially important to be with someone that brings out your best qualities, not your worst. You see, we all have good things about our personalities, as well as lesser positive things; so ensure that you are with someone that motivates you to reach your fullest potential, instead of holding you back.

It is up to you to act the same way!

Do not be a dream killer—be a dream builder.

You want the person that you are with to live a full and happy life. Do not be afraid or insecure about that fact. This life of ours is so precious, and we only get one chance here on earth; so care for each other, be loving and kind. Say nice things, and do not use harmful or hurtful words. Build each other up!

I once heard someone that I respect very much say that the secret to a long-term and happy relationship that will last and stand the test of time, is to simply "Try to out-love one another". I adore that concept! Try to out-love your mate and he will want to do the same in return. If he does not, it is then the simple to remember phrase that needs to come to mind: "Next!".

I am going to do my best to get you thinking, acting, and wanting MORE and expecting the BEST! You should NEVER "settle" and that means that you, in turn, have to treat YOUR MR. RIGHT, like a King, if you want to feel like a Queen.

Things to Avoid

Use your intuition to tell you whether or not a guy is really into you or right for you. Be honest with yourself, especially when red flags come up. Do not just overlook things because you are hoping for the best. Be real with your emotions.

Do not allow yourself to be taken advantage of, or to simply be a "booty call" for another's gratification or physical needs. Guys will never want to be with you long-term if they think of you as the *'go-to'girl*, when they are drunk and did not score at the club, or on their night out.

You have to have some appreciation and self-respect. When you do choose to be intimate with a man, it is also primarily up to you to protect yourself against STD's and unwanted pregnancy. Be aware and make smart choices BEFORE you do get involved with someone physically. It really is easy to make the right protection choices for your own health and life. ***Is it not a tiny, yet smart decision, worth safeguarding and be saving the rest of your life?***

Do not be one of these women who thinks that she can ensnare and trap a man by getting pregnant. This is cruel to yourself, the man, and most especially the child-to-be. This is not the path you want to take. If you really like a guy and he does not feel that way about you, pull yourself together and move on. It is not easy by any means, but it is right. The sooner you bring yourself around to this way of thinking, the faster you will heal and find a new path for yourself.

You will find the right person out there when the time is right for you.

You will also want to watch out for guys who do not want to introduce you to their family and friends. If they are not including you in social activities, consider this a warning flag and ask yourself—and him—why/why not?

It may not seem possible, but this is a tremendous sign of cheating or insincerity on his part. He may be married or already have a girlfriend who is not satisfying him completely. He could just be looking to line up a booty-call, or even be after a free ride, sponging on your money and means.

Be conscious about how men you meet behave. Is he proud to be seen with you? Guys that really are attracted—or even in love—have a hard time hiding it.

Do not lie to yourself to keep him in your life if he really does not want to be with you. If you are not getting the right vibe or connection, then have the courage to move on.

Do not let the great years of your life go by staying with the wrong guy just because you are afraid of being alone. Be honest about the relationship. Chances are that if you are not being treated the way you want, if you have to negotiate with him for his time, or if you are constantly trying to tell him how you want to be treated and what you are looking for in this relationship, then you are with a man who does not truly think you are the "one", but stays with you for more-or-less indulgent or selfish reasons.

Because of this, he is most certainly watching for his true "one" and when he finds her, he will be done with you and you will be left brokenhearted. One day you will wake up and ten years will have passed by that you cannot ever get back. Let self-honesty be your guide when deciding if you are currently with the right person for the right reasons. Start loving and valuing yourself *right now*.

It goes without saying that you should never allow someone to lay their hands on you, hit you, or hurt you EVER, whether physically, emotionally, verbally, even sexually. If this happens, get out RIGHT NOW and never look back. Such a man has extreme anger issues and character problems that you do not need to be a part of. You do not owe it to him to stick through it all with him.

You do, however, certainly owe it to yourself to get out while the getting is good. You are not a part of his therapy!

I think that today people jump into bad relationships out of a desperate need *"to be loved"*. Most do not even really look into if the person they are with has all the qualities that they are looking for. For example, you should really know before you decide to marry someone, what their financial situation and well-being is. (including debt!), You are about to sign-on for part of that load, obligation and/or debt—if there is any—so be smart and talk about it BEFORE getting serious, let alone married.

If you find yourself in a situation where you are engaged, then you should be able to openly talk about these things now, because if you cannot, it will certainly and assuredly NOT be getting any easier once you are married! (quite the contrary). Be open with him about where you are and stand financially, as well.

If you both have a lot of debt and a poor credit rating, then create an action strategy to get that debt paid down as much as possible and that credit score raised BEFORE you get married.

There is much more to be said about this topic. If you can create these goals and achieve them, then you have really proved that you can work well together as a team. Finances are among the leading cause for divorce, so be smart. You had best ensure that you do know what you are getting involved with and create that action strategy. You will be so far ahead of the game if you do this!

Do not just get married and then find out that he is still paying down a college loan, has massive debt and poor spending habits, or such related issues. Oh, yeah, and by the way, what if he recently filed for bankruptcy? Do not do that to your future! Pay attention now and to all of these details, ahead of time, BEFORE tying the knot! I cannot stress this enough!

Interesting Tidbits About Men

Things that men love about women:

- A confident woman that has a sense of style—they find this very alluring and sexy—stylish elegance

- A women who laughs a lot and has a good time—good-tempered

- A physically fit woman that takes care of her body—good physique

- A woman that also takes care of her nails, her feet and toes, her hair, and her skin—yes the physical is important but that does not mean you have to be a perfect size two to do any of these things, but *do* be well-groomed

- When women are positive and decide to build others up instead of tearing others down—encouraging, mature

- Women who are not naggers and complainers—up-beat

- Women who take responsibility when they make a mistake—humble and honest

- Women who are loyal and trustworthy, and who want the best for them—reliable and caring

- When you cook their favorite meal or foods, it makes them feel good and special! They love to be "cared for" just like we do, only in other ways. *(Even if you hate to cook, learn to make three meals that he likes, as well as a dessert that makes him smile. Chances are, once you learn those three, you will be more inclined to learn even more dishes, because he will show you so much appreciation that you will love the attention you get. If he does not appreciate it, then chances are that you are not with the right guy!).*

Things That Women Do That Drive Men Away Early On

So ladies, here are some of the things that you do that drive men away early-on and they do share these things with their male friends just like you do with the girls! It may surprise you, but it is true. (*Believe me, men chat it up too! They do talk about the way we act all the time*).

If any of these things apply to you, take notice, and make the necessary adjustments and corrections accordingly—DO NOT self-sabotage or undermine your own efforts and chance with the guys or Mr. Right!

The dating game is exactly what it seems like or appears to be: A GAME!

Depending how you play this game determines if you will win the man of your dreams (alias Mr. Right!) or be destined to live alone with way too many cats to count, thinking everybody else has it all wrong.

- Do you make too many calls and emails to him when you just met and are in the *getting-to-know-one-another* phase?

- Do you talk about all of your problems early on, letting him know right off the bat that you do not have it together? You make the first move thinking he will find that "sexy" when really you just killed the chasing game that men love to play. Ladies, they are hunters! Do not kill the excitement for them. Let them chase you. They love it! This is the best part for them. Work and play a little hard-to-get and challenge them. This does not mean treat them badly or break dates, but let them email *you* and call *you*! Let them take the lead and set up dates in the beginning.

- Do not call him at work and while he is out with his friends constantly—this makes you look insecure and needy.

- While out on your first date at dinner, offer to pay for your half of the bill. This will tell you a lot about the guy already. If he allows you to pay, then guess what, get used to it. If he refuses and picks up the tab, then he is a true gentlemen and most likely he will always be generous. You are not taking advantage here, but you are looking for all the right characteristics and there is nothing wrong with that. Plus, he will find it really sweet that you offered to pay and that you are not just looking for a meal ticket.

- Do not ask him too many questions about his Ex. Do not say "are you still in love with her?" or ask about what they did in the bedroom. Too many women obsess about the ex and previous relationships. The first thing you need to know is that *it is* his ex and that they are not together anymore, so quit bringing her to his attention all the time.

- Understand what he likes and do not try to drag him to things you know he hates. For example, he really might not want to go shopping with you. Most men hate shopping and he does not want to watch you spend your money on things that he find frivolous like "shoes". He has only three pairs and will never understand why you need 100 pairs. Plus, you are only showing him how you are going to be spending his hard-earned money if you were to get married or live together, and it will freak him out. No, he also probably does not want to go see the latest Chick-flick or tearjerker. It is simply just not his thing. That is what your girlfriends are for!

- Men do not like it when you do not think about, or understand the following things. During the months of August through January they are going to be very focused on, yes, "Foot-Ball Season", The

Play-offs, Superbowl and such related activities. That means college games are on every Saturday afternoon. Monday night football is like religion to them so respect it! Here is what you do: Get to know his favorite team and go online to check out who the star players are for that team. You may hate football, but your man loves it, so it would behoove you to learn about it just a bit. You may have to fake it.

Then he will find it really sweet and cute that you know the star players. You will gain major points and if you look at the schedule a week at a time, you can schedule events that are important to you around the games.

It does not cost or take much, a little effort all-in-all, but it will do wonders for you both! Let him come over to your place with a few buddies. Get them some great food and beer, leave for the day to go enjoy that *chick-flick* with your girl friends and hit the mall. You see, everyone wins! If you really want to score major points, take a look at who is winning while you are out then call him and say "YAY, your team just scored! Just thinking of you, go have fun with the boys." He will be eating out of your hand in no time flat!

- When he asks you if something is wrong and you say no, that is good enough for him. Men do not like getting into long drawn-out conversations as women do. They are not wired like women and do not work or think that way. YES or NO usually works well for them and they typically DO NOT make decisions that are "emotional" like we do. Try to understand the basics of how men think and tick, because it will serve you well all around, every time!

The Male Ego

The Male Ego is like a carefully placed, organized bookshelf. If one thing falls or tumbles, it can take down the entire towering whole!

The Male Ego is an enigma and utterly complex. First of all, you need to understand is that this is where men draw their self-confidence from. It is what makes them *men*, so to speak. If you start to build up that ego, you will get a lot further with them. Use kid gloves when you are talking about issues that men are sensitive about.

For example, DO NOT EVER compare them to the hottest Quarterback that just got a 50 million dollar deal. They feel pressure in many of the same ways that we do. They want to have six-pack abs, have women check them out, be funny, and they feel tremendous pressure when it comes to their career and financial capabilities.

When dealing with issues, always try to go at it from an angle that is positive. You do not want them to come to the conclusion (by themselves of course!), that you think they are a loser. When you use harsh words, it tears them down and their ego gets bruised. Yes, they might be more fragile and delicate than you, or that they want to believe or admit to! This is not to say that guys cannot handle hearing the truth or dealing with sensitive issues. They can. It is all about *how* you approach it and word it—it really is that simple.

Men want to be seen as "movers-and-shakers", like "The Donald" (Donald Trump). They want to think that every woman that looks upon them is very eager to 'sleep' with them, be a conquest, or serve them. This is the stuff or self-talk that goes through their head and thoughts. They want to think that they can have any woman at any time. They want to be seen as successful to you, to their peers and of course, to their families. If you understand the male ego, you will have a better sense of how to bring things up, start conversations and get what you both need in order to be happy.

Always build him up rather then tearing him down. If you do this, he will feel great around you. If you do not, then that woman at the gym that understands and embraces, utilizes and leverages the male ego, starts to stroke it regularly, will begin to catch his eye. This happens because she makes him feel good when he is around her. My advice? Rather let that person be you!

Never talk about his expanding waistline or receding hairline. If he is gaining weight and losing his hair, he knows it, and would be horrified to think that you also realize it.

Instead, decide to start walking together every day and use that time, not only to get exercise, but also to bond and talk about the two of you and your dreams and goals.

> **SIDEBAR:** My husband and I have done this for nine years with our three dogs. Every day we get up and do a long walk together. It gives us a chance to go through our day and keeps us close. Simple things like this add a lot of intimacy to a relationship. You can always find the time for this, even if it means watching less television or getting less time on the internet.

As I said early on, it is how you make them feel, not so much just the way you look. But imagine that now you are taking all of this advice, putting it into action, working out, looking and feeling great, you're positive and fun to be around when you're together, you build him up and laugh, and this, my dear friends, will get you to the altar faster then anything else. And when you do get there and become husband and wife, do not then get comfortable and slack off.

When you are a married couple, is exactly and specifically when you should treat one another *even better* than ever BEFORE. Ensure that you are having great sexual intercourse regularly and as often as you both feel comfortable with.

Be willing to experiment and get into trying new things together with one another. Keep up your appearance, so he tells you how beautiful he thinks you are, because you are! (not for what is in it for him!).

If he sees that you are still getting attention from other men, he will love it, knowing that you are his. Do not get comfy and start eating off his plate, calling him pet names that are derogatory and putting on the freshman… or newlywed 15 pounds. College is over ladies! You are now a married woman, so start acting like it.

Be hot and sexy for your man. Wear sexy lingerie to bed and take care of him. So when he sees those hot advertisements for Victoria Secret instead of having him think how hot the model is, have him think how hot *you* would look in that nightgown or skimpy ribbon-and-lace number. If you do this, he will be sure to return the favor!

I also want to add how important I think going to church is. Whether you believe in God or not, I want to encourage you that this is a good thing. I am a Christian and so is my husband. We find that it keeps us centered on the things that are important to us. It provides a positive atmosphere and keeps us both focused. This is also a great thing for the family. It has been proven that if a family that participates in the following, your success rate for a happy marriage increases tremendously. They are:

- Having dinner as a family at least five nights a week. This can include going out to dinner a few times, then cooking at home the rest of the time. Whatever you choose, it is keeping a time that is consistent daily and doing it with all members of the family in attendance.

- Going out with other couples regularly. Many successful couples have a date night once a week without the kids. You will need this to stay connected and get away, just the two of you from the pressures of home, work, life in general, that a young family can and typically does go through.

- If you have children it is great for the dad to feel as though he is part of their lives by coaching for a sports-team that the kids play on. Moms do so much and seem to have the kids more often, so this is a way that dad can also be involved and bond with the kids. Plus, you find out who their friends are and get to know other parents. This is also very important. The common theme is family. Here, EVERYONE has a role to play and as the wife, you really are the CEO to the family, even if you work, YOU set up how the family is to be managed. Doing things together and consistently so, is the most important thing.

If you do any, some, or all of these things, you will find dates much more easy to obtain, and great guys will start heading your way. I know the goal is to find Mr. Right. Just be clear that once you decide he *is* Mr. Right that you set out with a plan in place. A plan and future together to create your dreams while understanding that the other person's goals are also important. See if they fit in with what you want. Do not be afraid to tell each other your dreams and your fears. It is okay to be vulnerable. Just ensure that when you do open up about these things, that it is not on the first few dates!

These are intimate conversations that require a committed relationship and if you do not have that yet, you could scare Mr. Right away. So timing is everything! Listen to your gut and Ladies… just have a good time too, enjoying this process and have FUN!

All the things we talked about can happen for you. It is possible for you to meet your dream guy. Start working on YOU now and he will come to you. Be open to trying new things. Do not be close-minded or closed off to new ideas. Take chances and remember that life is a journey—one to be enjoyed.

Here is a unique perspective and way of looking at it…

PHENOMENAL WOMAN

—By Maya Angelou

Pretty women wonder where my secret lies.

I'm not cute or built to suit a fashion model's size

But when I start to tell them,

They think I'm telling lies.

I say,

It's in the reach of my arms

The span of my hips,

The stride of my step,

The curl of my lips.

I'm a woman

Phenomenally.

Phenomenal woman,

That's me.

I walk into a room

Just as cool as you please,

And to a man,

The fellows stand or

Fall down on their knees.

Then they swarm around me,

A hive of honey bees.

I say,

It's the fire in my eyes,

And the flash of my teeth,

The swing in my waist,

And the joy in my feet.

I'm a woman

Phenomenally.

Phenomenal woman,

That's me.

Men themselves have wondered

What they see in me.

They try so much

But they can't touch

My inner mystery.

When I try to show them

They say they still can't see.

I say,

It's in the arch of my back,

The sun of my smile,

The ride of my breasts,

The grace of my style.

I'm a woman

Phenomenally.

Phenomenal woman,

That's me.

WHAT YOU SHOULD LEARN
FROM THIS CHAPTER

Key-reminders and insights from Chapter 8 highlight:

- Even a man who is very interested in you will have **roving eyes**. There is nothing wrong with looking at an attractive woman—as long as looking is as far as it goes.

- Meeting Mr. Right **can happen anywhere**. Places as simple as grocery stores are wonderful for meeting new people.

- It is important **to look your best whenever you step out the door.** This does not mean that you need to spend hours on your looks to go buy milk, but it also means that you can not just fall out of bed and put on an old track suit. Being clean, well groomed and attractively dressed, means you care about the way you take care of yourself and how you look. It is a sign of confidence.

- It is important to **understand the male ego**. You can hurt a man's ego with a simple comment about hair or weight. Men know a lot of and about their flaws, and they do not need their noses rubbed in it.

- A relationship is not something that you can stop working on just because you get married.

Chapter 9

To Eat Or Not to Eat?
Eat! Just Do it Right!

Regardless of <u>where you live</u>, *big city or rural community*, or <u>your occupation</u>, *CEO or housewife and mother*, a **positive self-image** is essential to attaining personal happiness.

Throughout my career as a fashion and fitness model, I have met women from all walks of life and although their age, appearance and financial stature may have varied, there was always at least one common denominator. It is a pretty safe bet that if you talk to a woman about her appearance, she will tell you something about her body that she wishes she could change. When you stop to think about it, it is no wonder why!

First of all, we rely on the media to dictate the standard for what is considered beautiful and desirable. If we then fall short of their definition, our self-esteem takes a big hit. Whether you realize it or not, that poor self-image is ultimately reflected in other areas of your life, and in the long-run becomes an obstacle you must overcome to truly be happy.

It may seem unbelievable to you (the reader, audience) that people in my industry also fall victim to these unrealistic standards, but we do, sometimes even more so than people outside the industry.

The competition is fierce and I learned a long time ago that to be truly happy, I had to set and live by my own standards. I stopped comparing myself to others and no longer measure my success by someone else's yardstick.

I practiced what worked for me, what was healthy for me, and what made me happy, instead of falling into the media trap like so many of my friends and colleagues.

Set your own standards by evaluating what is important to you. I wholeheartedly support and encourage women who strive to reach their full potential, but I urge them NOT to lose sight of who they really are along the way. Instead of struggling to be someone else's idea of perfection, focus on your individual talents and strengths, working on improving those areas you would like to change and can change.

You may have your mother's thighs and your father's nose, you may not be 5'10", reed thin, or born with perfect hair and skin. Still, in no way should that translate to you seeing yourself as anything less than beautiful. It may sound cliché, but beauty truly is in the eyes of the beholder, and before others will begin to see you as beautiful, you must see yourself that way.

We have all met that one girl who acts totally and completely confident that we question in our automatic (inaccurate) thoughts "she is not even that pretty and she is heavy; what does she have to be so confident about"? Guess what, either she has totally understood her strengths and focuses on those, or she is a great actress. The point is, we can all choose to behave with confidence. She has made a decision to love herself, focusing on what she can do, instead of what she lacks. *__You go girl!__*

As a model, you learn this pretty quickly. Rejection is something you must get used to, yet still manage to muster the confidence to continue going out on job calls. Rather than giving in to self-doubt, as so many often do, I choose to focus on what I to refer to as my "inner-beauty". To help me stay centered, keep things in perspective, and never lose sight of who I really am as a person, I practice yoga and meditation and I continue to work on becoming a more spiritual, loving and accepting person.

The first step to discovering your own inner beauty is your acceptance of yourself. Love yourself, flaws and all, and focus on being the best person you can be: confident, strong, and happy. Now that's beautiful!

A GREAT EXAMPLE: JENNIFER LOPEZ

When talking about Jennifer Lopez, it would be easy to focus on her love life, since it has been so highly publicized—but this is not what I believe her true talent is all about.

Jennifer is much more than a woman who has had many boyfriends (or husbands for that matter). Sure she has had some difficulty finding true love the first few times around, and that is perfectly acceptable and fine too.

Instead, I want to focus on how remarkable her life has been. She truly came up from humble means to create a fashion and perfume empire, as well as making a name for herself as an actress, dancer, and singer. She has broken stereotypes with her electric curves and makes no apologies for the fact that she will never be—*nor does she desire to be*—rail thin. In fact, she declares that she adores her Latin roots and would not change a thing about her body.

Her famous backside has had many women flocking to the plastic surgeon's office in an attempt to get that famous J. Lo bootie. Let us look into the past and present of this incredible talent that is Jennifer Lopez.

Jennifer Lopez was born and raised in New York City's Castle Hill, a Bronx neighborhood. Born to Puerto Rican parents, she was always encouraged to learn to speak English, doing so clearly and comfortably. Her parents also stressed the importance of cultural assimilation, in order to properly blend in, so that she could function at her best in her life.

At the age of 17, Lopez' strong self-determination and sense of self-improvement, allowed her to finance her own singing and dancing lessons. Though she had enrolled at Baruch College, this was to last only one semester. Instead, Lopez juggled her time between working in a legal office, dancing classes, and her dance performances at night in Manhattan clubs. Her determination helped her through a period of months of unsuccessful dance role auditions, until she was finally selected as a rap artist's music-video dancer. This lead to a guest spot on the American Music Awards. Again, her determination helped Jennifer Lopez persevere. After having been rejected—twice—for the position as "Fly Girl" dancer on the program "In Living Color", she finally got the job. Soon enough, she was also the back-up dancer for Janet Jackson and appeared in her 1993 music video "That's the Way Love Goes."

Though she was contracted and scheduled into Janet Jackson's World Tour, she knew that she had to move on to her own things, and asked the superstar-singer to be released from her contract in order for her to pursue her dreams of acting.

Today, she has not only made it as a dancer, actress, and singer, but she is also the head of an enormous fashion and perfume empire, worth over 300 million dollars.

Throughout her entire life, Lopez has struggled with constant media attention, without a classic figure. Through this, and the media's never-ending scrutiny, Lopez has come out on top of it all, and has accepted her body because she is in great shape. She has a trainer in L.A. and takes Yoga classes in order to remain fit and toned.

Although she used to find it difficult to exercise, she now finds that it brings her balance of mind, body, and spirit. She does do some weights and cardio, but in a softer, more feminine approach. She stresses that she is in no way fanatical about her exercise regimen.

Lopez is now very proud of her body, knowing that she looks just like everyone else… not the latest runway model whose look is suited to her career, but to reflect the look of the average woman. She is happiest when she knows she is in top form, FOR HERSELF, and chides herself for occasionally slacking off—just like everyone else! (not unlike you and me!).

Jennifer also watches what she eats and adheres to a healthy diet. She knows what is good for her and what is bad for her, and tries to stay away from the bad things. Though she will occasionally indulge in a treat, she is not about to jump onto the next fad diet to lose the weight again. She is just a little bit more careful for the next while, when she knows she needs to regain her form again.

Lopez does not ban anything from her diet. She cuts neither carbohydrates, nor fats, nor sugars. What she does is eat in moderation, sticking to a balanced variety of foods. One thing that Jennifer is strict about is not taking drugs, not smoking, and not drinking—ever. Period!

Her supreme indulgence is to relax and spend some quality time to rejuvenate. She adores spa treatments, massage, and facials; though she does not do them all the time. These are a treat when the going has been especially tough. She also enjoys dancing, getting a good sleep, relaxing, and getting a healthy amount of sunlight.

Pre-natal health, nutritional excellence as well as a dedication to physical activities, matter and make a difference. J.Lo advocated for it all, particularly when she was carrying fraternal twins. She was not ashamed to show off her pregnant physique! Emme Maribel Muñiz, was born at 12:12am, weighing 5lbs 7oz and Maximillian "Max" David Muñiz, at 12:13am, weighing 5lbs 13oz, on February 22, 2008 on Long Island, New York by C-section.

When featured on the front cover of People magazine in the March 11, 2008 issue (they were then 4 weeks old), J. Lo was not returning to work until they were

15 months old and is now currently starring in "The Back-up Plan" (2010). She and her husband Marc are also celebrity part and co-owners of the Miami Dolphins. She is proud of who she is, how she looks, and how she chooses to live, with no excuses or apologies! If there is anything that we can learn from Jennifer Lopez, it is that we are all beautiful in our own way. The key to getting the most out of your appearance is to try to be healthy, and not forget to treat yourself on occasion.

In her own words…

"We've all had a love of our life and failed love affairs. I'm just the biggest romantic—it's really sad. I tell people that, but nobody listens.

I've always had a huge fear of dying or becoming ill. The thing I'm most afraid of, though, is being alone, which I think a lot of performers fear. It's why we seek the limelight—so we're not alone, we're adored. We're loved, so people want to be around us. The fear of being alone drives my life.

In every movie they want you to look as thin as you can look. In Selena, it was the other way around: "How can we shoot her butt so it looks like Selena's?"

I only do what my gut tells me to. I think it's smart to listen to other people's advice, but at the end of the day, you're the only one who can tell you what's right for you."

Part of my business is about being in shape and looking good. You can't lie to yourself about it. But I'm not the monster I used to be in the exercise department. You get past your 20s, you've got kids… you're kind of unmotivated. You want to be healthy and look good, but you want to do the least amount to maintain that.

STAYING HEALTHY AND FEELING VIBRANT

In addition to teaching me good social skills, an important lesson that my mother taught and showed me, was the importance of taking care of my body, especially my skin.

My mother has the most beautiful skin I have ever seen on a woman. She has passed her secrets on to me and I would like to pass them along to you, so that you may incorporate them into your daily routine. These are not new; they are very simple, yet I still know women today that do not take care of their skin. This will certainly help and is so easy to do!

A sense of physical and emotional well-being is something we all desire and I believe it is achievable for all of us—with a little effort.

Your skin needs to be important to you now, because as you age, the previous years of slacking on your skin-care will begin to show. That is why it is so important for good skin care to start today—so that tomorrow you will have a much healthier and more beautiful skin.

You need to make sure that every morning and evening you wash your face. Take off all of your makeup at night. In the evening, use a good eye cream and nighttime moisturizer. This will be different than the moisturizer you will wear during the day.

Find out what type of skin you have. Is it normal, oily, or dry? Chances are if you are anything like me, it is a combination of these things and more! Take the time to try new products and sample out what you think works best for you.

You certainly do not have to spend tons of money to get good skin care.

In the morning, get up and wash your face. Put on your under-eye cream and moisturize with a formula that also contains sunscreen—this is really important.

Then you are free to next put on your make-up. Ensure that you change your make-up pads regularly and clean your brushes gently with warm water and soap once a week.

On a daily basis, leave them out to dry overnight. This will help keep your skin cleaner and is more hygienic.

Most people forget to do this and it can create nasty bacteria that you are constantly putting back onto your skin every day! So, do clean those brushes and be sure to replace them once a year. I do this at Christmas time because that is when they have all the great selections to choose from and you can get great deals which is always good for the pocketbook and budget.

Food for Life

Before you get started making any radical changes to your diet, it is important to consult your doctor. After all, we are all different, and we will all react differently to dietary changes.

Even when you are taking "natural" and herbal treatments, you risk conflicts and allergies. You can make great changes to your diet, just make sure that you consult your doctor when you do.

You always hear that drinking water is the best thing that you can do for yourself, and I have to tell you I could not agree more. I drink water throughout the day.

To add some flavor and get a good dose of vitamin C, I like to add a pack of Emergen C to an ice-cold bottle of water. It makes the water taste great and I love the fact that I am getting lots of vitamin C.

I am a strong proponent of nutritional supplements and believe that taking vitamins and minerals should be high on your list of priorities in order to feel your best.

If you are lacking the vitamins your body requires, you are going to feel tired and worn-out, which could certainly lead to depression. Add a good multi-vitamin along with 1500 milligrams of calcium that contains magnesium to your diet and you are surely going to notice a difference.

It is also important that you get plenty of omega fatty acids. This will help keep your skin looking young and healthy and your hair soft and shiny. I also take a shot of liquid minerals each morning.

As women, there are important vitamins and foods that can help us feel great all the time… things like Soy, B12 and B6 for energy, plus folic acid, which is wonderful for women's' nutritional needs and physical well-being.

Black cohosh and evening primrose help maintain a healthy temperament, while we go through our monthly menstrual cycle. They can help with our emotional, hormonal ups-and-downs, as well as alleviating cramps associated with our period.

What you put into your mouth will determine how you feel. That is the rule of thumb here. It really is just that simple. If you become a lazy eater, you will get fat, feel tired and lethargic al the time. That is not to say that you cannot treat yourself to your favorite meal and dessert. But your over-all diet will determine so many things, including how you treat others. If you are eating too much sugar, you will become accustomed to it. You will find yourself and your body constantly craving more and more sugar.

If you eat a lot of salty foods, you will be bloated, and you will not be at your best, with no healthy glow. In order to feel and look your best, all areas of your life must be maintained.

Eat as close to nature as possible and maybe do one day a week that is all vegetarian. Cut back on the red meat. Incorporate fresh fish—all different types if you can. It is the healthier option. As some types of fish do have slight levels of mercury in it, it is important that you eat reasonable portions, and only one or two times every week. Though mercury levels in fish on the shelves are within the FDA's safety limits, you still do not want to overdo it.

Add lean turkey meat and buy organic as much as possible. This means for the meat products as well as the fruits and vegetables. If you cannot get what you want, or if you want to change the variety in your diet, change where you shop.

If you know the supermarket so well that every time you walk down a certain aisle, the bag of cookies automatically jumps into your cart, then skip that aisle! Change *how* you shop. You must be proactive when you are deciding to make a change. There are so many wonderful health-food stores across the country, that having everything you need to eat right and feel great is within easy reach and more affordable than ever.

Cut the Fast Food

If there is one thing in your diet that you absolutely do *not need*, it is fast food! Sure, it has its level of convenience for when you are on the run, but the consequences far outweigh any of the benefits it might offer.

The fact is that fast food just does not have the nutrition that you need in a well-balanced diet, but it does have an awful lot of other elements that you should never put into your body.

These include chemicals such as preservatives and flavor enhancers, sugars, sodium (salt), as well as an unbelievably high amount of trans-fats, one of the leading contributors to heart problems and obesity across the country.

There really is not any excuse for eating fast food. There are so many other wonderful foods out there that can be just as quick and easy to eat. It is more a matter of breaking the habit of going for the burger, fries, and soda, than actually finding something tasty and convenient.

The trouble usually starts in school. They offer fast foods because they are cheap and popular among the students. However, this sets up bad eating habits for those kids for the rest of their lives! This is why so many schools across the country and around the world are re-thinking their cafeteria strategies. It just makes good sense in the long run.

Do yourself a favor and break the fast-food habit in your life. Bring your own lunches, and keep them interesting, so that the temptation is never there to go elsewhere.

Alternatively get together with a group of five of your work-friends and have each of you supply a healthy lunch one day per week. This way, you will only have to make lunch once per week. You will have a surprise the other days, and you will always have something good and healthy to eat!

Balanced Eating

Of course, if you do not know what to buy, it will be hard to build a healthy diet for yourself. The key is not necessarily what you eat—it is what is *in* what you eat. You need to eat moderate portions, and know what your body needs, and how much it is taking in.

There has been an awful lot of press about cutting carbohydrates, cutting fats, and other efforts to lose weight. When it comes to maintaining a healthy diet, though, the key is not cutting things *out*; it is eating the right things in the right amounts, frequency and portions.

Making the decision to cut out certain things can be good for you as long as you understand why you are cutting them out and what you are replacing them with.

Your body needs certain basic building blocks, like fats, carbohydrates, and proteins in order for your body to be at its optimal health. It needs the input to give you its very best. Unfortunately, so many of us have terrible eating habits that we were raised with, that it becomes very difficult to change and we find that we lack the self-discipline to try something we know is good for us in the long-term. This is exactly why so many people yo-yo diet, going up and down in weight, with no real results.

What you need to do is make better food choices during the week, ensuring that you are cutting out those carbohydrates and added fats that are going to lead to more over-eating and binging.

Drink lots of water and stay hydrated, take your supplements, get your greens every day, eat several pieces of fresh fruit and have lean proteins on your menu.

Then on the weekends, you can reward yourself with a great meal out with a loved one or friends and enjoy a glass of wine, or a dessert. Maybe you love sushi. Well then, go for it! All in moderation of course! You have been good all week long, now you can indulge, a little bit at least. You see, the key here is watching yourself and being good most of the time. I am not a perfect eater all the time, not by any stretch of the imagination, but we can all try and make some small changes that add up over time on the positive side.

I try to eat as close to nature as possible during the week, like having lots of veggies and salads with homemade dressings made with fresh lemon, olive oil, and

186 CHAPTER NINE *To Eat Or Not to Eat?*

a bit of mustard. I mix it up and I love the taste. I also make sure that I eat oatmeal three days a week in the mornings and the other days I have egg white omelets, with veggies and soy cheese.

Then on the weekends I splurge (within reason and in moderation) and I enjoy myself. If I want chocolate, I have it. But I do not eat tons of it at a time. I have one or two bites and that is enough for me. I love meat! I wish I could be a vegetarian, but for me that does not work. I feel stronger and I have more energy when I eat meat.

So, I try to have red meat three times a month. The rest of the time I focus on lean-meats like turkey, fresh fish (all types) and organic chicken. Here is what I stay clear from: white and refined flours, that includes all baked goods. Now granted, I will cheat now and again and have cookies, (come on, give me a break, I am human too!!) but I am talking about the 90 % of the time that I am a clean eater.

Instead of eating carbohydrates loaded with sugar and starch like white rice and mashed potatoes, I try to eat whole-grains and brown rice and even then, I eat small portions of these things. To tell the truth, you really do not need a lot.

I use the "hand-rule" when it comes to portion-size and here is the rule: take a look at your hand. The inner part, called the palm of the hand, determines how much protein you will need at a meal. Next are your fingers. They determine your carbohydrate intake—that means both veggies and whole grains—so as you can see, you do not need a lot here. Your thumb represents the fat that should be in your meal.

With this in mind, use your hand as a cheat-sheet type guide and a visual reminder when you sit down for your meal or load your plate. If your meal is bigger than your hand, take half of it home and eat it later. If you do this, you will lose weight and keep your weight stable without going up and down. These are simple things that I do to keep myself lean and strong.

It is not enough to think, you have to be healthy as well. If you do not have enough energy and you find that you are always tired, most of the time your diet is the problem. You are eating all the wrong things. Take this opportunity to turn those bad eating habits around today.

Clean out your fridge and pantry. Donate the food that you have or give it away. Stop buying food from the market where you currently shop; instead find a new health-food store to shop at that can offer you great treats that are healthy.

Believe me, these stores have all the food in them that you will need and you will not be tempted with things that you do not really need. Sometimes you have to change your routine to get the desired results that you want.

Now let us take a closer look at what these foods are all about and how you can incorporate the good ones versus the bad ones, putting the right things in and leaving the wrong or harmful ones out of your diet.

Fats

Dietary fats are important for good health. This may sound a bit far-fetched, if not outright strange, but it is true. As far back as 1929, dietary fats were found to be "essential" in our diet. Balance is the key to making fats work for you and your body. There are two important considerations:

- Consume a variety of good fats. *These include unrefined oils, such as extra virgin olive and safflower and sesame. Fats from butter, meats, eggs and dairy are good as well, as long as they are part of a balanced diet.*

- Avoid hydrogenated (or partially hydrogenated) fats. *These include margarine and many of the fats used to make breads and other products (read labels). Hydrogenated fats can disturb the metabolism of fats in the body. Also, fried or cooked fats should be avoided for similar reasons.*

Why are fats so good? Here are ten reasons:

1. Source of energy

2. Essential to supporting the hormonal system

3. Natural insulator

4. Supports and protects your body from strain and damage

5. Vital for proper prostaglandins cell function

6. Regulate your vitamins and minerals

7. Essential to your health and that of your baby during pregnancy and lactation

8. Help protect your body against the harmful effects of x-rays

9. Important to proper digestion

10. Tastes good, making a meal worth eating!

Fat is important for good health. Dietary fats, however, must be balanced, to include a variety of natural oils, butter, meats, eggs and dairy in moderate amounts.

Many people avoid fats because of misinformation and fear. As time goes on, the "low fat" trend will disappear, as much research has already shown the benefits of this necessary, healthy substance.

Carbohydrates

Carbohydrates take the form of sugars, oligosaccharides, starches and fibers. It is one of the three major macro-nutrients which supply the body with energy (fat and protein being the others).

Whereas it is important to maintain an appropriate balance between calorie intake and expenditure, scientific studies suggest that:

- A diet containing an optimum level of carbohydrates may help **prevent body fat accumulation.**

- Starch and sugars provide **readily accessible fuel for physical performance,** (just make sure you get these are in small portions).

- Dietary fiber, which is a carbohydrate, helps keep the **bowel functioning correctly.**

- Apart from the direct benefits of carbohydrates for the body, they are found in a wide range of foods which themselves bring a variety of other important nutrients to the diet. For this reason it is recommended that carbohydrates be supplied from **diverse food sources** to ensure that the overall diet contains adequate nutrients.

- Carbohydrates are needed for the central **nervous system, the kidneys, the brain, the muscles** (including the heart) to function properly.

- Carbohydrates are important in **intestinal health and waste elimination.**

- It is also important to remember that carbohydrates contribute to the taste, texture, and appearance of foods and help to make the diet more varied and enjoyable.

Carbohydrates are the macro-nutrient that we need in the largest amounts.

According to the Dietary Reference Intakes published by the USDA, 45% - 65% of calories should come from carbohydrates. They are mainly found in starchy foods (like grain and potatoes), fruits, milk, and yogurt. Other foods like vegetables, beans, nuts, seeds and cottage cheese contain carbohydrates, but in lesser amounts.

Carbohydrates in all shapes and forms are good for your health. They can help to control body weight, especially when combined with exercise, they are vital for proper gut function, and are an important fuel for the brain and active muscles.

Proteins

The building blocks of protein are amino-acids. When protein is eaten, your digestive system and processes break it down into amino-acids, which pass into the blood and then are carried throughout the body. Your cells can then select the amino-acids they need for the construction of new body tissue, anti-bodies, hormones, enzymes, and blood cells.

Protein is not one substance, but literally tens of thousands of different substances. The essential amino-acids must be consumed in the diet, because the body does not make them.

The complete proteins that contain the eight essential amino-acids come from meat, poultry, fish, eggs, milk—all dairy, cheese and soy. They are basically anything that comes from the animal side of the spectrum. Nuts and legumes (peas and beans) contain some but not all of the essential amino-acids; (these are known as incomplete proteins).

Proteins are necessary for tissue repair and for the construction of new tissue.

Every cell needs protein to maintain its life. Protein is also the primary substance used to "replace" worn-out or dead cells:

- Most white blood cells are replaced every ten days.

- The cells in the lining of the gastrointestinal tract and blood platelets are replaced every four days.

- Skin cells are replaced every 24 days.

- More than 98 percent of the molecules in the body are completely replaced each year!

Your muscles, hair, nails, skin, and eyes are made of protein. So are the cells that make up the liver, kidneys, heart, lungs, nerves, brain, and your sex glands. The body's most active protein users are the hormones secreted from the various glands—thyroxin from the thyroid, insulin from the pancreas, and a variety of hormones from the pituitary—as well as the soft tissues and hard-working major organs and muscles. They all require the richest stores of protein.

It is important to understand the value of protein in our diet. Protein is the best nutrient to eat in order to maintain an even blood sugar level because it is metabolized over a long period of time. Protein can be converted to glucose if need be, to fuel our engines in a manner of speaking.

Things to Help You Feel Great

- **25% Water** (Reduce caffeine intake and try to eliminate soft drinks and fruit juice).

- **25% Strength training** (To stay toned and young—your bones will thank you later in life and you will burn more calories per hour when your body has more lean muscle mass).

- **25% Cardiovascular exercise** (You need this to keep your heart healthy, burn calories and keep up your level of endurance. This should be done three to five days a week, for a minimum of 30 minutes every time. If you want to lose weight, I recommend six days a week for 45-60 minutes: walking, running or cycling. My personal favorite is kick-boxing)

- **25% Rest and recovery** (This should be the most relaxing, quality time you give to yourself. You need to get a solid eight hours of sleep and your muscles need the recovery time. This is a great time to treat yourself to some time away or at a spa, or at the very least a hot bubble bath and salt rubdown, which is inexpensive and something you can do to yourself. Your skin will feel like a million bucks!)

A regular routine of all of the above will add balance to your life **and** help you to feel your absolute best. Putting yourself first is not selfish at all. If you take care of YOU (for once, as well as on a regular basis), you will do a better job of taking care of your family!

I also like to incorporate a relaxing workout like Yoga or Pilates into my schedule, at least once or twice a week. This will help with mental focus and give you time to reflect on your goals. I sometimes go with a friend or my mom or sister, giving us some special "girl-time" together.

Regular exercise and a healthy diet will undoubtedly help to make your skin glow, but there are other things you can do as well to help keep your skin clear, smooth and soft. *(For those of you reading this who may be in your twenties, I urge you to start taking care of your skin now. If you develop good habits now, you're sure to reap the rewards of your extra efforts as you age!).*

Healthy Inside and Out

Like everyone, I love a good tan, but I am also very aware of and concerned about risks like sun damage. Thank goodness, there are so many great self-tanners on the market that you really do not have to spend time in the sun to get great color.

When looking for a self-tanner, my advice is to purchase a product that goes on with color, so you can see if you have missed any spots.

I recommend using an exfoliating product in the shower before you apply the self-tanner. You can buy a salt or sugar scrub at any department store, drugstore or even health-food store. They make some with great fragrances. *(To save money, mix your own with equal amounts of sea salt and baby oil. It works wonders!)*

I also use a bristle brush on my skin for increased circulation. This is especially helpful if you sit at a desk all day. You will need something to create extra circulation in your hips, thighs and bottom. Make sure you brush your skin in upward motions going toward your heart and keep the brush dry. I like to do this before I get in the shower and exfoliate. Do this and your skin will feel baby soft. After exfoliating, you are ready for the self-tanner and are just minutes away from a deep, dark tan.

I use a self-tanner twice a week, and to avoid dry skin I always remember to moisturize my body every evening with a creamy lotion rich in emollients, like avocado, vitamin E and cocoa butter.

Now, let us talk about your hands and feet. Whether you do them at home or go to a salon, manicures and pedicures are a must! That does not mean just changing the polish. That means smooth cuticles, nails trimmed and filed, and your feet always looking sandal-ready.

As I said before, men love soft, sexy feet. I make sure that I put lotion on my hands and feet every night. In fact, I apply hand lotion every time I wash my hands. Keep a small tube in your purse. This will help keep your hands looking young. Getting your nails and toes done is also a great way to pamper yourself! Indulge and splurge a little!

If you are blessed with perfect teeth, then you should do everything possible to keep your smile beautiful. I make sure that I get my teeth cleaned every six months and I floss daily. There are so many teeth-whitening products on the market today, in all price ranges, that there really is no excuse for your smile not to be bright. A beautiful smile is something people will always remember about you.

Remember that looking and feeling your best is a combination that comes from feeling good BOTH on the inside AND taking the steps that will keep your physical body healthy and fit. If you do these things, then you will also feel good about yourself on the outside. Take the steps that are outlined this chapter and be the best *you* possible.

Below are some of my favorite recipes… if you do not know how to cook, this is a great time to learn! Like you, I also love eating out, but it is very difficult to maintain your weight if you are eating out too often.

Go online and look up some of your favorite things to eat and teach yourself how to make them. You may be surprised at how much you enjoy the process. If you eat at home more often you will stay leaner because you are in total control of how you prepare your food. It will also ending up costing you less money. When you do decide to go out to eat, you can really splurge.

This book is about helping you find the balance in all areas of your life. I wish you all the health and happiness that I know you deserve. If you are good to yourself, others will be good to you.

INSIDE TARA'S KITCHEN

Savoring the aromas, tastes and textures of foods is one of life's greatest pleasures. Eating healthy never has to mean denying yourself a pleasure this great. You just need to have some nutritional *know-how* and some really great cookbooks.

These are some of my favorite recipes. These, and more can be found in the *The High-Protein Cookbook* by Linda West Eckhardt and Katherine West Defoyd (Clarkson Potter Publishers, New York, 2000). ** These recipes and others from health-minded cookbooks can help you properly balance your nutrients while enjoying zesty, palate-pleasing gourmet meals.

Garlic Lime Chicken

Marinating chicken breasts with the flavors of garlic and lime creates a delicious contrast in flavors. When the chicken is cooked on an outdoor or indoor grill, the charred grill marks, which are the caramelized sugars in the meat, give this chicken a touch of sweet and sour. Ideal to serve on top of a vegetable purée.

Countdown:

Preparation time: 5 minutes

Marinating time: 20 minutes

Cooking time: 10 minutes

What You Need:

- 2 tablespoons low-sodium soy sauce
- Grated zest and juice of 1 lime
- 1 teaspoon Worcestershire sauce
- 1 garlic clove, minced
- 2 boneless, skinless chicken breasts (10 ounces total), split and pounded to ¼ inch thickness
- ½ teaspoon cracked black pepper
- ½ teaspoon mustard

Directions:

Combine the soy sauce, lime juice and zest, Worcestershire sauce, garlic and mustard in a glass dish or reseal-able plastic bag. Add chicken and turn to coat with mixture. Cover the chicken and refrigerate for 20 minutes.

Remove the chicken from the marinade and pepper it thoroughly. Discard the marinade.

Preheat a grill or skillet over medium-high heat. Brush with olive oil. Cook chicken until golden on both sides, opaque and cooked through, about 10 minutes in total.

Serve hot or at room temperature and garnished with additional lime zest.

Nutritional Analysis:

- 302 calories
- 11 g. fat
- 44 g. protein
- 3 g. carbohydrates

Cooking Lesson:

Sometimes half the battle is won with patience. Just let the chicken swim along in this aromatic marinade, and the flavor will be so much better.

Menu Suggestions:

You can afford a sweet temptation with this meal. Buy or make sugar-free meringue shells and serve alongside ½ cup of berries. You'll have added only 3.5 grams of carbohydrates with the meringues and 5 grams or so with ½ cup of raspberries or strawberries.

Salad Niçoise with Citrus

This quick salad from the French Riviera is filled with olives, tomatoes, asparagus and tuna. You can add any other greens or left-over vegetables. These ingredients were chosen to give a variety of textures, colors and flavors: crisp, pale green lettuce; ripe, red tomatoes; soft, pink tuna; and dark green asparagus. Use this recipe as a base and create your own version of this classic.

Countdown:

- Make dressing
- Blanch asparagus
- Assemble salad

What You Need:

- ¼ cup red wine vinegar
- 2 tablespoons Dijon mustard
- ¼ cup diced red onion
- 2 tablespoons water
- 2 tablespoons olive oil
- Salt and freshly ground pepper to taste
- 2 (6-ounce) cans low-salt, soft pink tuna packed in water, drained and rinsed
- ½ pound fresh asparagus
- 4 cups washed, ready-to-eat field greens or French-style salad
- 2 medium tomatoes, cut into wedges
- 8 pitted black olives, quartered

Directions:

To prepare the vinaigrette dressing, whisk the vinegar and mustard together in a large bowl, with onion and water. Whisk in the oil to a smooth consistency. Season with salt and pepper, to taste. Flake the tuna into the vinaigrette.

Cut or snap off the 1-inch-long fibrous base of the asparagus and discard. Slice the remaining asparagus into 2-inch pieces (you should have about 2 ½ cups). Bring a medium saucepan of water to a boil.

Add the asparagus. As soon as the water comes back to a boil, drain the asparagus and refresh in cold water. (If using thick asparagus, boil 5 minutes.)

To microwave the asparagus instead, place asparagus in a microwave-safe bowl and microwave on high for 4 minutes. Add the asparagus to the tuna mixture and toss gently. Divide the lettuce between two plates. Spoon the tuna-asparagus mixture over the lettuce. Arrange the tomato wedges around the plate, sprinkle the olives over the top and serve.

Makes 2 servings.

Nutritional Analysis:

- 424 calories
- 51 g. protein
- 14 g. carbohydrates
- 20 g. fats

Citrus:

- 2 medium oranges.

Divide the oranges between two plates and serve. Makes 2 servings.

Nutritional Analysis:

- 62 calories
- 1 g. protein
- 15 g. carbohydrates
- 0 g. fats

Helpful hints:

Use the dressing recipe provided here or purchase a no-sugar-added oil-and-vinegar dressing and add diced red onions.

Turkey and Asparagus Penne Salad, with Tangerine and Orange Yogurt

This turkey, asparagus, tomato and basil pasta salad can be assembled in the time it takes to boil water and cook the pasta. My first experience with whole-wheat pasta was a surprise. It has a nutty flavor, very good texture, and can be used like regular pasta.

Countdown:

- Cook pasta
- Prepare turkey salad
- Prepare yogurt and tangerines

What You Need:

- ½ cup whole-wheat penne or other short cut pasta (2 ounces)
- ¼ pound asparagus
- ½ cup sliced carrots
- 1 medium tomato, cut into 1-inch cubes (1 cup)
- ¼ pound sliced smoked turkey breast
- ½ cup fresh basil, snipped with scissors
- 3 tablespoons no-sugar-added oil-and-vinegar dressing
- Salt and fresh ground pepper to taste

Bring a large saucepan filled with water to a boil. Add pasta and cook for ten minutes, or according to package instructions. (Do not overcook).

While the pasta is cooking, cut or snap off the 1-inch-long fibrous base of the asparagus and discard. Slice the remaining asparagus into 1-inch pieces (you should have about 1 cup). Add the asparagus and carrots for the last two minutes of cooking. Drain. Place the pasta, asparagus, carrots, tomato, turkey and basil in a bowl. Add dressing and toss well. Season with salt and pepper if desired and serve warm. Makes 2 servings.

Nutritional Analysis:

- 334 calories
- 23 g. protein
- 26 g. carbohydrates
- 15 g. fat

Tangerine and Orange Yogurt:

- 1 cup light orange-flavored yogurt
- 2 medium tangerines, peeled and segmented

Divide the yogurt into two dessert bowls and top with tangerine slices. Makes 2 servings.

Nutritional Analysis:

- 87 calories
- 5 g. proteins
- 18 g. carbohydrates
- 0.2 g. fat

Helpful hints:

- Whole-wheat pasta can be found in the pasta section of most markets

- A quick alternative to chopping basil, is cutting it with scissors

- To save time and saucepans, add carrots and asparagus to pasta while cooking

Stir-Fried Chicken on Bitter Greens

Think of this as a Thai-style entrée. Finish your meal with fresh melon or berries.

Countdown:

- Preparation time: 15 minutes
- Cooking time: 15 minutes

What You Need:

- 4 cups bitter salad greens (any mixture of watercress, arugula, Belgian endive, bok choy, spinach), rinsed and spun dry
- 1 tablespoon rice vinegar
- 2 boneless, skinless chicken breasts (10 ounces total), split and pounded to ¼ -inch thickness
- ½ onion, sliced
- 2 tablespoons oil

Sauce:

- 1 garlic clove, pressed
- ¼ teaspoon sugar
- 2 tablespoons dry sherry

Compose the greens on two dinner plates and drizzle with vinegar, then set them aside.

Whisk together the ingredients for the sauce in a small bowl.

Cut the pounded chicken across the grain into 1-inch wide strips.

Heat a skillet or wok over high heat, then add the oil and onion. Stir-fry until the onion edges begin to brown. Scoop the onion into a bowl and reserve.

Add the chicken and stir-fry until it begins to brown on the edges and is thoroughly opaque and cooked though, about 2 minutes.

Scoop the chicken into a bowl with the onions.

Add the sauce mixture to the wok and stir to free any browned bits. Return the chicken and onions to the pan and stir until the sauce cooks down, about 3 minutes more.

Spoon over greens and serve immediately.

Nutritional Analysis:

- 395 calories
- 47 g. protein
- 7 g. carbohydrates
- 18 g. fat

Cooking Lesson:

Use the Asian technique of cooking everything in the same pan—just not at once—and you will get the crisp-tender, flavorful results you love when you eat out. It takes practice and a lot of attention. Do all your cutting ahead of time; get the necessary bowls and props around you. You will soon be sure to love this technique!

WHAT YOU SHOULD LEARN FROM THIS CHAPTER

Key-reminders and insights from Chapter 9, highlight:

- Your health is extremely important to **your overall ability to enjoy life**, as well as to your capability to express how beautiful you really are inside and out.

- What you eat has an impact on your physical, mental, and emotional self, so, since you are what you eat, you should eat **only the healthiest and tastiest foods** so that you are healthy, happy, and beautiful.

- Women today have to give 100% of themselves just to maintain their busy, multi-tasking lifestyles. This 100% is made up of **water, strength training, cardiovascular exercise, as well as rest and recovery.**

- Taking care of your body on the outside is just as important as taking care of the inside of your body. Set up a healthy routine for **hygiene and personal care**, to make yourself feel and look better.

- **Eating healthy** is neither hard, nor time-consuming. Nor is it even expensive, as long as you have **the right recipes**. Purchase one or two really great healthy recipe books to enjoy the best in your life.

Chapter 10

Full Circle

"The only thing constant in life is change."

—François de la Rochefoucauld

You have now learned much about all of the vital steps that you can take to live life to the fullest, from discovering who you are and knowing what you want from life, to living a healthy lifestyle, and even money management.

But how do you turn all of these concepts into a plan that you can actually use?

That is really the key-question, the core of what we need to do: SYNERGIZE! Put it all together.

That is what this chapter is all about; taking everything that you have learned and applying it to your life to become the happy, healthy, well-rounded person that you want to be.

30-DAY TRIAL UNDERTAKING:
A GETTING HEALTHIER ADVENTURE

The true test of any new lifestyle habit that you are trying to develop is in the "30-day trial" concept. Just like with "as seen on TV" products that so often advertise their 30-day guarantee so that you can test the product without risking losing your money if it's a lemon, you can also try new self-improvement habits for 30 days BEFORE you go all-out, go with gusto, for the full version!

The one GOLDEN rule however is: that for those thirty days, you need to dedicate yourself to your techniques and goals, and not cheat once. *(After all, you are doing this for you! If you do cheat on your self-improvement efforts, you are only cheating yourself out of the results that you want so badly!).*

Remember, it is the first few weeks of establishing a new habit—whether it is eating healthy, starting an exercise program, writing in a journal, or sticking to a financial budget—those are the most difficult. By sucking it up and sticking to it for the first 30 days, you will already be past the hardest part and will have built up some inertia, which makes it much easier to keep going! Take my word for it… it gets easier!

The reality is that we do really self-sabotage or trip ourselves up sometimes. We psyche ourselves out of getting started, by mentally thinking about the change as something permanent—BEFORE we have even begun. It seems too overwhelming to think about making a big change and sticking with it every day for the rest of your life. This holds especially true when you are still habituated to doing the opposite.

The real catch-22 is: The more you think about the change as something permanent, the more you stay put!

But what if you thought about making the change only ***temporarily***—say for 30 days—and then you are free to go back to your old habits? That does not seem so hard anymore.

Exercise daily for just 30 days (nothing extreme, even a walk will do), then, use what you have learned about your exercise habits to form a schedule that works best for you.

Stick to healthy meals for 30 days, then when you have discovered that there are lots of tasty, healthy options out there that do not take much time to prepare, make some decisions for treating yourself every now-and-again.

Write in your journal for thirty minutes every day for 30 days, then you will know how much time you really do need for writing in your journal, and when you enjoy it the most.

Could you do it? It still requires a bit of discipline and commitment, but when you set a goal of only 30 days to start—as a trial run—it is not nearly so daunting as making a permanent change. Any perceived deprivation is only temporary.

If it will help you, you can also count down the days to achieving your goal. And for at least 30 days, you will gain lots of benefit. It is not so bad. You can handle it. It is only one month out of your life.

Now, if you actually do complete a 30-day trial, what is going to happen?

First, you will go far enough to establish it as a habit, and it will be easier to maintain than it was to begin it.

Secondly, you will break the "addiction" cycles and entrapments of your old habit during this time.

Thirdly, you will have 30 days of success behind you, which will give you greater confidence that you can continue.

Finally, you will gain 30 days worth of results, which will give you practical feedback on what you can expect if you continue, putting you in a better place to make informed long-term decisions.

Therefore, once you hit the end of the 30-day trial, your ability to make the habit permanent is vastly increased. But even if you aren't ready to make it permanent, you can opt to extend your trial period to 60, or 90 days.

The longer you go with the trial period,
the easier it will be to lock in the new habit for life.

Another benefit of this approach is that you can use it to test new habits where you really are not sure if you would even want to continue for life. Maybe you would like to try a new healthy diet, but you do not know if you would find it too restrictive. In that case, do a 30-day trial and then re-evaluate.

There is absolutely no shame in stopping after 30 days if you know the new habit does not suit or help, or work for you. Odds are that you will not need to stop altogether, you just need to have another look at the way you are approaching the new habit, and do it in a different way. Your way. No harm, no foul!

This 30-day method works best for daily habits, but there is nothing that says you cannot use it for a habit you want to build 3-4 times per week, such as a cardio workout. It can also work well if you apply it daily for the first 30 days and then cut back thereafter. This is what I would do when starting a new exercise program, for example. Keep in mind that daily habits are the easiest to establish, so it is always better to start out with a daily habit that you can cut back on, instead of trying to build up, from fewer days per week.

Here are some examples of tasks that you can take on every day, in order to build new habits that will help you with your self-improvement and journey to a better, healthier you, body and lifestyle:

- Eat breakfast

- Start each day by telling yourself—out loud—what a great day it will be

- Write in your journal

- Spend quality time with yourself

- Take steps to get to know yourself better

- Work on your latest goal

- Phone someone in your support group for a good, comfortable talk

- Try something new

- Shower, do your hair, and put on make-up

- Eat a very healthy meal

- Go for a walk

- Do Yoga/Pilates

Certainly, there will be dozens of other things that you can do to improve your life in 30 days, based on what you have discovered in this book. The power of this approach lies in its simplicity. Even-though doing a certain activity every single day may be less efficient than following a more complicated schedule—weight training is a good example because adequate rest is a key component for success.

You will often be more likely to stick with the daily habit. When you commit to doing something every single day without exception, you cannot easily rationalize or justify missing a day, nor can you promise to make it up later by reshuffling your schedule.

My best advice: give trials a try!

Positive Changes

Of course, you will only be able to benefit from your 30-day trial periods if you have prepared properly. Give yourself a month—call it a 30-day *pre-trial* period—to get yourself and your life set for your habit-building trials.

This time can include anything you need to get done to ensure the success of your trial habits.

For example, if you intend to eat **at least one healthy meal every day**, clean out your kitchen, throwing out (or donating) all of your junk food, and find a store where you can regularly buy fresh, healthy foods.

To prepare for your **daily exercise routine** you will want to make sure that you have weights for your strength training, the right pair of shoes (and perhaps a video) for your cardio, and a yoga mat for the Yoga or Pilates you will be doing once or twice per week. *(Or, you may find it easier to work out at a gym where others can motivate you and you can try some new classes. Gyms today want your business, so shop around and you will be certain to find a place where you can join for a low fee. It will be money well spent.)*

Since you will be **writing in a journal every day**, go out and buy yourself a notebook that you will find comfortable to write in. Spiral notebooks work well, since they fold back on themselves, and they don't spring closed when you are not holding them open with your non-writing hand. Look through the different notebooks and journals in your local stationary or office supply store and find the one that will motivate you the most.

SIDEBAR: I love to find pretty journals because I am a girly-girl and it makes writing more enjoyable for me when my book has a pretty cover and watermarked pages. I make a full relaxing and therapeutic experience out of my journal writing. I love to make a pot of my favorite tea and take the time to relax with my thoughts. It is a very comforting ritual for me and the process is something that I look forward to every day.

Start thinking about the different goals that you want to achieve, and begin writing out certain points for achieving those goals. You may not know every single point, but it will give you extra time to think, during which you can fill in the blanks.

Make your 30-day trials as smooth as possible by preparing in advance.

This will give you much better odds of success, and will give you a better chance for building those good habits in an effective and positive way.

Create a 'Habit-Building' Environment

Make sure that you are happy in your space. This means that it should be a clean space in which you feel comfortable and yet still motivated and productive. (All-right… you do not necessarily need to be able to eat off the floors, but get rid of dirt and clutter!).

Create a space of love all around you. Just the colors, accents, and organization of your home can make all the difference in your outlook on life. This does not mean that you need to make massive renovations if your home is not perfect.

What it does mean is that you need to make sure that your home—or at least one room in particular in your home—is a place where you can go to be happy. It should not contribute to feelings of sadness, frustration, or depression. It should make you feel better as soon as you walk in the door!

This has been critical for me, especially while writing this book. In that light, I painted my office dark green. Of course, you are probably now thinking that I do not have any taste at all. It is true, many people do not like the color green, let alone use it in their office as a wall-color, or they consider green to be a "kitchen" or "bathroom" color (since it is considered to be a color of cleanliness, freshness, and health). However, although everybody does have a similar reaction to each color, we also each have our own special and very personal reactions to each different shade of color.

Dark green gives me a sense of power, so I thought that it would work well in my office. But as I worked in the space, I found that I did not like how I felt, so I decided to re-paint it to my favorite color: pink. I hung gorgeous chandeliers and added a black-and-white pony hair chair. Now the space makes me feel completely loved! It is customized and to my own personal style and liking, I might add. Others might not like or 'see' it, but for me it is PERFECTION!

I have fresh flowers and plants in my office, (the fresh-cut flowers, usually on a weekly basis). They are straight from my garden, picked by my husband, for me, because he knows how much I love flowers. It makes me very happy. I have also included my favorite scented candles and a small fountain.

I have created an environment that inspires me. You can, too. Below, is a list of things that can get you started in creating your "space of love".

Create the space of love all around you with these **seven simple steps.**

1. **Color**—this can be anything from the walls to furniture, throw pillows, to rugs.

2. **Lighting**—you may enjoy a room with a beautiful hanging chandelier, or prefer the flicker of soft scented candles.

3. **Life**—add your favorite plants and flowers to a room to bring life to your home, and lightness to your mood.

4. **Sound**—create your music library with all your favorite songs on your cd player or I-pod. But do not just store the music, play it throughout your home!

5. **Snooze**—fresh new sheets and bedding (400 thread count and up are the best). You want a soft, comfortable bed that keeps you cool in the summer and warm in the winter. For extra comfort, give a featherbed a test drive!

6. **Accessories**—shake things up a bit. Try putting new covers on your throw pillows, or get new matching "everyday" dishes. Nothing too expensive; just something different and special.

7. **Prepare**—if your home is ready to entertain, you will do it more often! Make sure you have all the entertaining essentials, such as

a bottle each of red and white wine, great wine glasses, martini glasses, and everything you need to make your favorite martini. Pretty paper napkins and swizzle sticks can also spice up that little get-together.

All of these things can be done at reasonable cost. You do not need to hire an interior decorator. Sometimes just changing your furniture around, painting a wall, adding flowers and beautiful candles to a room, can instantly make you feel better! What a pick-me-up! Give it a try...

Start small and begin to watch decorating shows that might just inspire you! You do not have to spend a fortune; keep your eyes open for great finds at antique stores and discount stores. Treasures abound!

With such a space around you, you will be ready to take on the world, and all of the great positive changes that you have lined up for your life!

Tips for Getting Started on Your 30-Day Plan

Here are some additional tips to help you to get off to the right start for your *30-day plan.*

- Get a calendar. Stay on track, monitor and follow, count down the days (Also to mark your progress on!)

- Write out your 30-day action goals. Here's an example below:

  - Wake up and proclaim "today is a great day and something wonderful is going to happen to me today."

  - Pray. "Thank you, Lord, for my health and for this day. Protect me and keep those that I love safe. Thank you for everything you have done in my life."

- Turn on the morning coffee and while it brews, write out your goals, affirmations, and your to-do list for the day.

- Get ready for your morning workout.

- Exercise. Cardio minimum of three days a week, strength-training three days a week, and yoga or Pilates to help relax. Make a schedule to suit this model.

- Work out. Each workout should be 45 minutes in length for the best results. Make sure you start each workout with a good stretch and end it with a stretch. This is the key to not getting injured.

- Come home, shower, change, and eat.

- Eat breakfast. Eat a healthy meal that will provide you with energy. Protein is especially important. Try egg whites (4 with one yolk then a half of cup of oatmeal with Splenda for sweetness and maybe a bit of soymilk.

- Plan your meals. Take your daily vitamins and minerals, and if you take your food to work even better, because you can take control of what you are eating. Make sure to eat a large green salad every day, with lots of colorful fresh veggies. Watch out for hidden fats and added calories in dressings. You can make great ones yourself and stick them in the fridge.

- Have good snacks on hand, such as fresh veggies. You can pack healthy snacks and fruits: apples, oranges, grapes, and throw in some almonds. A healthy, low-fat yogurt is great for women.

Drink lots of water. Watch the caffeine intake, and cut out fruit juices or soft drinks (diet soda is alright, as long as you limit it to no more than one per day).

- Dinner should be a nice small salad, fresh veggies, and a four-ounce piece of protein. If it is chicken, try to buy organic. Work with several different types of fish each week. You can still have red meat, just limit your intake to a maximum of once per week. Try to add turkey to your program as well. Once you get used to eating like this, you will love it and you will feel inspired by your new-found energy.

- During the evening, it would be great for you to take a nice warm (not hot) bath, when you can find the time. Instead of watching hours of TV, read for 15-20 minutes from a book that will teach you something new. Try to make it something that interests you and that you will enjoy, but also something that you will be able to use in your life.

- It is nice to take an after-dinner walk; especially if you have dogs because remember, they need their exercise to.

Try to repeat these habits for 30 days. You can create your own schedule. Though you may not be able to get to your workout in the morning with your current schedule, you may have to do it after work, or even get up an hour earlier, in order to accomplish this goal.

If that is the case, you will also want to go to bed an hour earlier, so you can still get those 8 hours of sleep that we women need (and love) so much.

The bottom line is that you are trying to create a new, better life, by way of a new, better program for yourself. You can do it! Just try it and see!

A FINAL NOTE

Living a happy, resilient, and optimistic life is wonderful, and is also good for your health and longevity. Being happy actually protects you from the stresses of life.

Each of us has the power to make the changes that are necessary in our lives. Even if we find ourselves in an unbearable situation, we can always find solace in the knowledge that it, too, will, can and MUST change!

Support groups and great relationships are essential to happiness. Happiness is actually found in everyone. Increasing it is a way to make a life more wonderful and also healthier, more balanced, rewarding and satisfying.

Now that you have read this book, it is not hard to understand why so many people claim that being happy is easy; all you have to do is decide to be a happy person! In fact, it was Abraham Lincoln who said ***"Most people are about as happy as they make up their minds to be."*** The choice is simple really, *choose* to be happy.

Think about it—you already have so much to be thankful for! God has granted you many great gifts, and you should not take these gifts for granted or lightly. Make the effort to be happy in your life, taking advantage of all that has been bestowed upon you. Then start by making it better with your own contributions! One step at a time, one day at a time… for 30 days and then beyond!

Live your life and be bold. Our world needs you and all of your gifts and talents! Make this precious time here on earth an incredible one because you only get but ONE chance to make it great!

About the Author

Tara Brooke is a savvy lady in business as well as in her personal life. She has always had a tremendous amount of drive; the kind of ambition that has enabled her to move mountains in her life.

Having come from humble beginnings, Tara put to use all her talents to make her dreams a reality. Even from the age of nine she had big dreams, knowing that she wanted to carve out a better life for herself, believing that with hard work and strategy she could turn her luck around and "have it all". She describes her younger years growing up as "the best and worst thing that happened to me" as during that process, a lot of painful learning that took place. Life isn't always easy but we can make and create our own happiness. It's really up to us!

Between the ages of 18-22, Tara was already achieving her childhood dreams of working as a professional model which, in turn, led to her becoming a high profile spokeswomen for some of the biggest names in the nutrition industry. She was the national model and spokeswoman for MetRx and was named the first "Ms. MetRx". She also worked as a model-spokesperson for EAS as well as for Med-pro International. She then starred in three work-out DVD's of her own creation and realized that it was through the power of her thoughts she was able to get this far and be well on her way to success.

Tara Brooke then met her own Prince charming who literally swept her off her feet. She is a devoted wife and mother to twins while on a personal level, she continues to push ahead on her path to becoming her own personal best! Her passion now is to show younger women of this generation that no matter what their status or circumstances may be, they too CAN HAVE IT ALL! She is committed to show others how they can subscribe to the highest standards of excellence, to work smarter, and be determined to achieve their own goals and their dreams. Encouraging others comes naturally for Tara who is now excited to watch her book "Beautiful Ambition" take off to soar and inspire others to strive for even greater heights.

Bonus

I want to take a moment to thank you for reading my book. It is my sincere hope and joy that within the pages of my book you are able to create and realize your dreams for your future. That you will allow your dreams to soar and that you will step out in boldness and pursue the things you want without fear and without setting limits on yourself. The world is yours for the taking!

My wish is that you will reach for the stars and find a love so deep it takes your breath away. That every day you are able to appreciate the beauty in this world and are encouraged then to give back to others. Each one of us has special talents within us that can help and enrich the lives of others. Don't keep these gifts to yourself, but share them! Everything that is beautiful and wonderful starts with a thought, an idea followed by a determination to make this day your best day yet.

I encourage you to visit my website www.tarabrooke.com. On these pages I will continue to motivate you and provide you with excellent tips and suggestions that can be put to use every day. So, be a part of my blog. Write in. Ask questions and I will answer them. I am doing what I love and I believe that motivating and encouraging others is my greatest gift. It is my absolute pleasure to help provide the tools and insights that you can put to use every day in your life.

Thank you again and here's to your success!

Tara Brooke

BUY A SHARE OF THE FUTURE IN YOUR COMMUNITY

These certificates make great holiday, graduation and birthday gifts that can be personalized with the recipient's name. The cost of one S.H.A.R.E. or one square foot is $54.17. The personalized certificate is suitable for framing and will state the number of shares purchased and the amount of each share, as well as the recipient's name. The home that you participate in "building" will last for many years and will continue to grow in value.

Here is a sample SHARE certificate:

HABITAT FOR HUMANITY

THIS CERTIFIES THAT

YOUR NAME HERE

HAS INVESTED IN A HOME FOR A DESERVING FAMILY

1985-2005

TWENTY YEARS OF BUILDING FUTURES IN OUR COMMUNITY ONE HOME AT A TIME

1200 SQUARE FOOT HOUSE @ $65,000 = $54.17 PER SQUARE FOOT
This certificate represents a tax deductible donation. It has no cash value.

YES, I WOULD LIKE TO HELP!

I support the work that Habitat for Humanity does and I want to be part of the excitement! As a donor, I will receive periodic updates on your construction activities but, more importantly, I know my gift will help a family in our community realize the dream of homeownership. **I would like to SHARE in your efforts against substandard housing in my community!** *(Please print below)*

PLEASE SEND ME _____ SHARES at $54.17 EACH = $ $_____

In Honor Of: _____

Occasion: (Circle One)   HOLIDAY   BIRTHDAY   ANNIVERSARY

    OTHER: _____

Address of Recipient: _____

Gift From: _____ *Donor Address:* _____

Donor Email: _____

I AM ENCLOSING A CHECK FOR $ $_____ PAYABLE TO HABITAT FOR HUMANITY OR PLEASE CHARGE MY VISA OR MASTERCARD *(CIRCLE ONE)*

Card Number _____ Expiration Date: _____

Name as it appears on Credit Card _____ Charge Amount $ _____

Signature _____

Billing Address _____

Telephone # Day _____ Eve _____

PLEASE NOTE: Your contribution is tax-deductible to the fullest extent allowed by law.
Habitat for Humanity • P.O. Box 1443 • Newport News, VA 23601 • 757-596-5553
www.HelpHabitatforHumanity.org